What Did You Learn at Work Today?

The forbidden lessons of labor education

"Helena Worthen skillfully weaves the theories of how people learn with real life experiences of workers she's interacted with, both in the classroom, on the shop floor and on the picket line. Anyone aspiring to worker education will find this book invaluable." **Mike Matejka, Legislative Director, Great Plains District Council, LIUNA**

"Worthen has produced a wise book springing from the important but mostly overlooked idea that workers can use their workplaces as a place for collective learning...Worthen has melded down to earth stories of working people with theories of learning that attempt to explain their successes and failures in terms that might be useful for workplace and community activists." **Fred Glass, Director of Communication, California Federation of Teachers**

"Helena Worthen has used her experience as a labor educator to help explain how workers learn, adapt, improve and defend jobs that are often poorly planned, organized and executed while staying alive literally and figuratively. This is a book I didn't know I needed to read!" **Mike Sacco, University of Illinois Labor Education Program, retired IBEW Local 21 Business Representative**

"Worthen's examples of learning... are an intimate look at how collective knowledge is learned and produced by working people, whether on the job or on strike...lessons rarely appreciated, let alone mined for their value to understand and improve the human condition. [it] takes her into groundbreaking territory, where very few U.S.-based educators, scholars or labor organizers have gone before. And we are richer for it." **Teresa Albano, Co-editor, People's World, Mondo Popular**

DEDICATION

To Nancy Augustine, whose courage made other people brave, and Penny Pixler, General Secretary Treasurer of the IWW (1987), in gratitude for her example of a life well-led.

What Did You Learn at Work Today?

The forbidden lessons of labor education

Helena Worthen

HARDBALL

PRESS

This is...

A book about work, at a time when there are too few jobs;

A book about labor at a time when hardly anyone belongs to a union;

A book about what you already know;

A book about learning that explains how you did it;

A book for working people, for teachers, and for the labor movement;

A book for everyone who has ever asked, *"Can they get away with that?"*

TABLE OF CONTENTS

CHAPTER 1:
WHAT DID YOU LEARN AT WORK TODAY?

Maybe you learned how to run some new software. Maybe you learned how to drive another vehicle. Or how to sauté onions, how to thread a needle while it's still moving, or how to lay out the equipment you may need in a hurry. Maybe you learned how to approach a new project or how to assemble a light fixture. Maybe you learned how to record the results of an experiment or stack containers so they don't tip over.

Maybe you learned how to take a nap during your break. Maybe you learned how to make a meal by scooping food off the plates coming back into the kitchen. Maybe you learned how to text your kid with your hand in your pocket so no one could see you using your phone, to see if she made it home from school.

Maybe you learned something about your employer. Maybe you learned that he likes to hear that you really love your job.

Maybe you learned that if you take a day off to go to your sister's wedding, you'll get fired. Maybe you learned that instead of hiring another person to work with you all night at the convenience store, the company will put in a security camera so they'll have a movie of you being killed in a holdup.

Maybe you learned that the spill you've been directed to clean up with a mop is actually something that should be cleaned with special vacuum equipment while you wear a hazmat suit.

Maybe you learned that when you do your work really fast you may get a bonus but you may get injured, and so might others who try to keep up with you. Maybe your co-worker explained that to you.

Maybe you learned that if you work more than forty hours

a week, there's a law that says you're supposed to get paid time and a half. Maybe you learned that the person working next to you has heard that too, and thinks you're right.

Maybe you learned that you have a union, or that you don't have a union, or that you have a union but it is no good, or that if you say the word "union" out loud, your clock is ticking.

Some of these lessons are things your employer will teach you. You may even get paid to learn some of these. Others you have to find out by yourself. Some of them will get you fired. Some will save your life. Some will save the lives of other people.

All of these are knowledge; things that have to be learned. Learning is a process. It is what creates knowledge. Knowledge is deep. It is heavy. It is political. It is emotional. It is collective, meaning that it is shared by many people. No one owns all of it. It is broad and powerful, but only if the people who share it are organized.

This book is about the lessons you learn at work and how you learn them. It is written for three groups of people. The biggest group is people who work, including high school students who work while going to school. The second group is people who know something about labor history and unions. The third group includes teachers, especially adult educators and teacher educators. Teachers of course are also workers.

So whether you are a high school student with a part-time job, or an older worker with a job that you have had for a long time, a labor movement activist who already knows a lot of law and history, or a teacher who has any of these people in her class, this book is for you.

CHAPTER 2:
KNOWLEDGE AND CONTROL

"Can they get away with that?"

My phone rang in my office. A woman said she was calling on behalf of her mother. She asked, "Is this the Labor Department?" I told her no, we're the Labor Education Program of the University of Illinois.

We get a lot of calls like this. People search online using the key word "labor" but don't actually know what they're looking for.

Unlike most callers, however, this woman was almost incoherent, and her mother was even worse. I could hear her mother weeping and shouting in the background. The mother, apparently, had lost her job. The woman said she'd call me back later when her mother calmed down.

Most of the time, they don't call back, but this woman did. Their story went like this.

The mother and father worked in a car dealership that also ran a repair shop. The mother worked in the office and the father was a mechanic. They had been there many years. The mother had been complaining to the employer that the office was too hot and stuffy. The employer told her to just keep the door open so the cold air from the repair shop could blow through. However, this being Chicago and winter, the cold air was too cold, and worse, the fumes from the repair shop were giving her a headache. She complained again. Now the owner told her that he wasn't going to do anything else for her, and that if she kept on complaining, she was obviously not suited for the job. After a few weeks of headaches she did complain again and he fired her. Not only that, he fired her husband.

The way he fired her husband was by getting the old man to

sign some papers saying he had voluntarily quit. However, the old man was actually unable to read – he was illiterate - and was not aware of what he was signing. All this time, while the two of them were working at the same place, his wife had been covering for him by doing whatever reading had to be done. He had not, however, asked her to read these particular papers. Now that both she and her husband had lost their jobs, they had also lost their health insurance, which was employer-based. Unfortunately, the old man had prostate cancer and had been relying on his health insurance to pay for the treatments.

The daughter told me this story because the mother was still too upset to talk. I could hear her in the background, sobbing and trying to interrupt and explain. The daughter asked me, *"Can they do that?"*

Can they do that? is the question that we hear over and over again. Ninety-nine percent of the time the answer is, "Yes." The first thing Eve realized after she bit into the apple was that she and Adam were naked. The first step of knowledge for people who work for a living is to realize that they are naked, too—naked in the sense of having no protection: "They can do that."

Why hadn't this woman and her daughter ever learned that?

It is helpful to make a quick comparison between school learning and learning at work. Schools are set up so that people can learn. While many schools are badly set up and no one learns, or are set up to be gatekeepers so that only a few students learn, *few will deny that schools are for learning.* That's why we give them money. Work is not set up that way. Its purpose is different. Work is set up to make a product or provide a service, whatever it is. If you get training, you get trained enough to do that. Any additional learning that happens is on your own. Answering this woman's question, "Can they do that?" will not help the employer manufacture the product.

"They can do that" means that unless you have representation through a union, workers in the United States are "at will" employees, meaning that the employer's "will" is what rules.

There are a few exceptions. If you can prove that you are being discriminated against on the basis of race, color, sex, religion, or nationality, which are "protected categories" under Title VII of the Civil Rights Act of 1964, you can file a charge with the Equal Employment Opportunity Commission (EEOC). But in order to win one of these cases you need to demonstrate that the treatment you received as an individual is motivated by your employer's prejudice against the whole category of which you are a member. This is hard to prove.

If you are over forty, you may be able to charge age discrimination, but that is also hard to prove. If you are part of an attempt to organize a union, you can argue that the employer is retaliating against you for your union activity. But then you have to prove that the employer knows that you are participating in union activity. This is also hard to prove.

The state of Montana actually passed a law in 1987 that created some limits on at-will employment. However, the whole notion that you can't be fired for "no reason," or that no one can fire you for something like wearing a silly necktie or just looking unhappy, is wrong. They can. Simply because something is "not fair" doesn't mean it is illegal.

In other words, this woman and her husband were in big trouble, and our system of employment relations provides them with no legal recourse.

This story does not have a second chapter. It is not one I can use to show how people fight their way back out of such a situation. The bad news is that individuals fighting alone have very little chance of winning. When you combine the arbitrariness of employment relations in the United States, the extreme inequality of power in the workplace, and the fact that a job is sometimes more valued for its access to healthcare than for a paycheck, these things all work together to kill people. This story is unusual only in the particular cruelty of the terminations and the profound grief felt by the mother when she found out that her husband had signed his own resignation papers. It may take a while for this older couple to actually die as a consequence of this loss of their jobs, but that is probably what will happen.

However, there are places where people can learn the answer to the *Can they do that?* question, along with its consequences for workers. In some places you can learn it in classes with a teacher. Labor education programs in the United States, for example, address the question. They are typically sited at community colleges or land grant universities, where they do outreach to working people and the labor movement just as agricultural extension programs do outreach to farmers. This is the kind of school in which I teach. And learn.

"Not for a hot minute"

The Labor Education Program at the University of Illinois has offices on the ground floor of a building near the Chicago Loop. The room in the center of the offices is a classroom. It's 6:30 pm on a dark winter night with snow on the sidewalks and twinkly lights in the trees. The classroom is brightly lit. Flip charts, a coffee pot, students sitting at tables. They are adults, all sizes and shapes. Their jackets and coats make a big wet pile on the floor in back. I am the teacher.

The class I am going to describe is one I loved. It had workers in it from all different kinds of workplaces – bus drivers, electricians, nurses, clerical workers, custodians, park rangers, postal workers, truck drivers and others. There were also two stationary engineers. Stationary engineers are part of the Operating Engineers union and run enormous stationary mechanical systems, like skyscrapers.

The class was working on an exercise based on a famous event that took place in the 1980s at an auto assembly plant in Lordstown, Ohio. Workers in the paint shop at the plant noted an electrical problem. The newly installed meters that controlled the heat to bake the paint onto the cars were not operating correctly. Things were getting too hot. Too hot meant that an electrical fire could start, complete with explosions. They contacted the supervisors, who said the meters had been tested after installation and were fine. The problem continued through the shift and into the next shift, despite continued attempts to persuade management to take action. Finally, the workers shut down the paint shop. Cars started backing up throughout the plant. Upon coming to work, the morning shift found the entire plant in gridlock. At that point, the technicians from the company that installed the meters were called to the plant. They found that the meters were in fact set incorrectly, and fixed them.

The exercise was supposed to be about what steps to take when something is going wrong at work and why these particular workers had to bring the whole plant to a halt in order to get their problem addressed. However, the discussion never got that far.

When the narrative of the work stoppage at the auto plant had been explained, one of the stationary engineers slammed his hand on his table and said, "That could never happen!"

Since it had happened, I looked at him and waited to see what he would say next. One of the reasons I'm telling this story now is to show how much students in labor education classes learn from each other, as compared to learning from the teacher. That also means that while the teacher has to prepare a curriculum, she also has to be ready to stand back and let some unexpected teaching and learning take place.

"It could never happen," he repeated. "That's what they

pay us for. If I think something needs to be fixed, no one argues with me. Not for a hot second."

The other engineer, a young man who runs one of the biggest skyscrapers in the world, nodded.

My first reaction was to refer to their training, which involved long apprenticeships paid for through the union-based apprenticeship program. These training programs are challenging, competitive and costly. Electrician apprenticeship programs, for example, invest over $50,000 to train each apprentice over a five-year period. The break-even for the union will only come after years of work and pennies-per-hour-of-work contributions to the training fund.

However, I was interrupted.

"What did you say?" asked one of the school teachers, looking at the engineers.

"What do you mean?" said another teacher, in an incredulous tone of voice.

The engineer turned to look at her. "I said, they pay us to know how things are supposed to be done. If I say something isn't working, it all stops until they do what I say."

There were three teachers in the class. The third was shaking his head. All three of them seemed flabbergasted.

I asked them to tell their stories.

One was a literacy instructor. He had run a literacy program at the Cook County Jail. It is widely known that when people who are incarcerated get some kind of education, especially literacy or basic skills, their chances of gaining employment, or at least staying out of jail upon release, are greatly increased. His program had just been cut.

One was a high school biology instructor. She taught at three different schools. She had to pack up what more or less constituted a biology lab – an aquarium, bottles of chemicals, a box with a microscope and slides – and put it in the trunk of her car and load it and unload it at the three different school sites where she was supposed to teach biology.

The third was a social work teacher. She had part-time jobs at different places, one at a community college and one at a private university where she had MA students. She noticed that the community college didn't have any counselors. She volunteered to set up a counseling program using student interns from her MA program, under her supervision. She set up the program, using a classroom that was going unused for one-on-one meetings between students and counselors. To give them privacy, she put some cut-out brown paper over the window in the classroom door. The school administration told her that this was prohibited due to the need for surveillance to prevent crime. They said this was non-negotiable. The counseling program died.

All these teachers had college degrees and MAs. Did their long years of education give their knowledge power in their workplace?

"I know how things are supposed to work," said the biology teacher. "I know what a biology lab looks like and what kids need in order to learn something about life on earth. Does anyone listen to me?"

The literacy instructor said the same thing. The social worker actually got so mad that she walked out of the classroom to go have a cigarette in the parking lot. When she came back, she was brushing snow off her sweater.

You don't get paid for knowing how it should be done if that's not how you're supposed to do it

There are many theories about the relationship between knowledge and work, most of them about why some workers are paid more, some, less. Some of these theories include: white men are paid more than women or African-Americans; people have to be paid more to do dangerous jobs; jobs that require lots of training receive higher wages; jobs where a strong union can bargain for the workforce pay higher wages; jobs where you are handling valuable commodities like diamonds or investments— or skyscrapers—pay a lot.

For a while in the 1990s and early 2000's, there was talk about "the knowledge economy," as if people would automatically get paid more for knowing more. According to this theory, high-wage workers must know a lot because the market, being fair, automatically matches what they can do with what they must be paid.

This is ridiculous, but people fall for it. Obviously, you can know a lot and still be paid very little. The three teachers in my class were shining examples of both. But for example, in the US Department of Labor *Report on the American Workforce 1999*, wages were actually used as a proxy for skills. Jobs were categorized as low-skill or high-skill. If a category of workers got paid high wages, they were listed as high-skill no matter what they actually did at work.

The importance of that moment in class is that people from very different occupations were suddenly confronted with evidence that some workers, as a workforce, took for granted their power to control and manage their work, even to the point of being able to call a halt to what was going on if they thought it was not being done right. Unlike the workers in the auto plant, the stationary engineers' knowledge of how things ought to be done controlled how their work was done.

It's not only jobs that require years of training that have this power. There are jobs that you can get hired into that require no training but are good jobs, where workers have organized to make decent wages, work safely without being harassed, and wield the power to use what they learn about their work to improve the jobs and protect themselves at work. Most of these started out as bad jobs but were turned into good jobs. But making a bad job into a good job is not easy. This is what really requires knowledge.

There is learning theory that explains how workers learn to organize to make bad jobs into good jobs. There are programs like ours, in Illinois, and others around the country, where these lessons are captured, taught and shared. But overall, this knowledge is not well recognized, despite the fact that it saves lives. In some places it is called "oppositional" knowledge; in others, "resistance" or sometimes "consciousness." In many places, opportunities to create and learn this knowledge are attacked. We will talk about all of this.

Questions that ripple out in circles

In the first chapter of this book I asked, "What did you learn at work today?" I suggested different things that someone might learn. Now I want to choose one specific situation and think about the kinds of questions that might, or should, arise from that situation.

Let's take a worker at a plant where cleaning takes place. Cleaning happens in most workplaces: vats get cleaned, tools get cleaned, industrial laundry gets cleaned, fuel and vapor get cleaned. The chemicals that are part of the cleaning process are numerous, expensive, often severely toxic, and sometimes hot or pressurized. They are all supposed to be listed on a poster required by the Occupational Safety and Health Administration (OSHA), according to a law passed in 1970. This poster is supposed to be somewhere visible to everyone, but it is often hidden in a closet or missing.

So here is a worker and there is a spill, and the worker is told to clean up the spill. The worker has safety glasses and gloves. The simplest thing to do is to get a mop and a bucket, start mopping, and dump what's in the bucket down a utility sink into the sewer system. His supervisor has given him a direct order. If he doesn't obey, he exposes himself to being disciplined. He could be fired, suspended, demoted or yelled at. What should he do? Here is the start of a list of what he needs to know in order to decide what to do:

What is the substance on the floor?
What could it do to him?
What equipment does he really need?
Should he dump it down the sink, or should he do
something else with it?

These questions address the immediate physical reality in front of the worker doing the cleaning. The answers to these questions should be common knowledge in any workplace. But often they aren't.

Then come more questions he needs to be able to answer.

Does his supervisor understand the risk?
How far can he trust his supervisor's knowledge
of the risk and his supervisor's willingness to put
the worker at risk?

These questions are not just about his personal relationship with his supervisor and his willingness to trust that individual. They are also about the integrity of the whole workplace.

What kind of training do his supervisors get?
Are they accountable to anyone?
Who supervises them?

If the worker has doubts about his supervisor's competence or respect for worker safety, he needs to think about other things, too:

What are his legal and contractual rights if he
refuses to obey a direct order?
What will happen to him if he refuses to mop up
the spill?
Who else will stand with him? How should he

communicate with those other workers? How far are they willing to go?

Then he has to think beyond that particular job:

What would life be like for him if he loses his job? What is at stake for him personally and individually?

A safety question is always a good place to start when talking about what a worker needs to know. At first we're dealing with straightforward questions of toxicity and exposure that invariably have answers. But quickly we face the next level of questions about legal and contractual power, trust between the worker and the supervisory structure, trust among the workers as a workforce and the overall social relationships of the workplace. All these involve knowledge. All this is learned.

The importance of this cannot be overstated: The US Bureau of Labor Statistics reports that in 2012, nearly 4,700 people in the US died on the job. Our fatality rate (3.2 per 100,000 workers) is five times higher than Great Britain's (0.62 per 100,000 workers) according to their Health and Safety Executive.

The questions about the social relationships of work are just as relevant to the worker's decision as the questions about what the spill is and what equipment he needs.

When a serious accident happens, we read interviews with the family of those involved and we hear about how those considerations were weighed. The wife of the sole survivor from the 2006 Sago Mine disaster told a newspaper reporter that she and her husband, who was disabled in the accident, knew the mine was unsafe, but he chose to keep on working because the alternative – the wife going to work – would incur babysitting costs that they couldn't afford. So the couple weighed the risk of going down in the mine against the price of a babysitter.

The worker who stands near a pool of unknown substances, mop in hand, trying to decide what to do, is similarly not just thinking about what the stuff is, but about his co-workers, his relationships, and the rest of his life. He has to choose. What he chooses will depend on what he's thinking.

"Readiness"

Knowledge about the social relationships of work can be learned and shared by our students in our labor education classrooms no matter what their line of work, because it is not specific to any one *kind* of work. It is a dimension of *any* kind of work. Nurses, electricians, bus drivers, postal workers, teachers, construction workers, and clerical workers would all recognize these lessons. They are lessons about how a job should be done, how to do it safely, how to communicate with other workers, and how to pass on a safe and secure workplace from one shift to another. The lessons would include a history of the fight that took place to achieve each of these. A custodian who makes one dollar over minimum wage can teach these lessons to an office worker making forty dollars an hour.

If this knowledge was just about producing a better product, management might welcome it. But since it is also about making a bad job into a good job, from the point of view of the worker who is trying to make a living, it is rarely welcome.

Everyone in the class that snowy night in Chicago could identify with the frustration that comes from lacking the power to do a job right without defying orders and risking discipline. They knew what it was like to not have the right tools, staff, equipment or opportunities. They all empathized with the auto workers who could tell how hot the paint shop

14

was getting and were trying to warn the supervisors. They described similar situations on their own jobs:

The charge nurse knew she was setting up a risky situation when she scheduled an oncology nurse on a pre-natal ward in order to cover a shift.

The pharmacist assistants, who worked at a very old hospital where the equipment was deteriorating, knew that when the pill dispenser jammed and prescription pills spilled out onto the floor, they were sweeping up and throwing away medications worth thousands of dollars.

The bus driver whose route had been extended the whole length of the city knew that by the time he got to the farthest neighborhoods, he would be behind schedule.

The letter carrier knew that when mail gets sorted mechanically she would have to check much of it visually, which would keep her out on her route until sundown.

The teacher who changed her lesson plan from teaching a class of twenty to crowd control in a new class of thirty-five knew that too many of his students would be left behind in the big class.

Welfare caseworkers, who once had caseloads of two hundred and now carried over a thousand clients, knew that client phone calls would be bouncing around the office in an infinite circle because no one had time to pick up. They also knew what their clients were suffering.

But who listens to the people who actually do the work, to find out how it should be done to get it right and to make the job itself decent, fair, and survivable? No one – unless the workers have the power to make themselves heard.

The good news is that workers can learn how to control their jobs. However, this lesson is not learned the way things are typically taught in school, where individual students are provided with information, rehearsed, then tested and moved from one level to another up a predetermined stair-step system. Learning to control one's job differs from school-based learning in every way imaginable. It is also not "workplace literacy," which was a popular topic in the 1980s and 1990s, as our economy moved from a base in manufacturing into hi-tech, at least temporarily. At that time, laid-off manufacturing workers were being retrained as computer repairmen, cable TV installers or healthcare workers. It was assumed that what these workers needed was a basic literacy program when what they needed more was a class in workers' rights. Nor is it a "skill" in the sense that many policy makers talk about skill training and skill gaps.

One of the main ways in which these lessons differ from school learning is that they are collective. They are shared, in the sense of "class consciousness," an awareness of and openness to the other people who understand things from your perspective. This is why they are best learned in classes or informal gatherings where people meet and talk to each other. Another word that captures their character is "readiness": a state of being prepared, awake and aware, fully equipped, in touch with one's allies, ready to go, ready to fight if necessary. Still another word is "forbidden." This word reveals that these lessons are learned in the middle of a fight. In spite of the fact that they can make the difference between an abusive workplace or a decent workplace, a sad life or a decent life, or even life and death, this knowledge is the target of many strategies to make it hard to get, hard to pass on, and hard to learn.

The next chapter, called "Forbidden Lessons and the Anti-Union Industry," will provide examples of obstacles or choke points where this knowledge and opportunities to create it are blocked, attacked and distorted, both outside and even within the labor movement.

CHAPTER 3:
FORBIDDEN LESSONS AND THE ANTI-UNION INDUSTRY

"Is that legal?"
— question sometimes asked of labor educators when we explain that we teach organizing, among other things

The daughter of the older couple who had been fired from the auto dealer asked, "Can they do that?"

How is it possible that an adult, who has a bank account and a driver's license and pays taxes, who may own or rent a home and manage it, who has raised children and sent them to school – in other words, carries out the minimum busywork of adulthood – can't answer that question?

Why don't they teach this in high school? Or better yet, middle school, because by the time people are in high school, most of us are working part-time, mowing lawns, stocking groceries, serving food, sweeping floors or recycling? If we're not working, we're looking for work.

The answer is that this knowledge is not merely secret, it is actually forbidden. In the next pages, I will identify some of the choke-points that cut off the movement of information about the right to organize and even the right of assembly, found in the First Amendment in the Bill of Rights of the US Constitution. Because I have worked in labor education programs that provide this kind of information, I will include ways that these programs are undermined or blocked. These range from failures to fund and implement state laws requiring labor studies curriculum in the public schools to harassment and direct attacks on programs, teachers and researchers.

What happens to labor education programs, of course, is just the tip of the iceberg. The fear of what might happen if workers got together and tried to take control of their work goes way back.

Adam Smith: Meetings end in conspiracies

Adam Smith, the author of *Wealth of Nations*, the first comprehensive book about economics in the newly-industrialized world of the 1770's, had no doubt that whenever people from a particular trade or line of work got together they would waste no time in figuring out how to improve their lives as workers:

> People of the same trade seldom meet together, even for merriment and diversion, but the conversation ends in a conspiracy against the publick, or in some contrivance to raise prices (Smith p. 129).

"A contrivance to raise prices" means a contrivance to get higher wages. Of course this is only "against the publick" if you don't include the workers in the public.

Giving advice to his readers, in all probability the owners of capital who employed many such tradesmen in their factories, he warned:

> It is impossible indeed to prevent such meetings, by any law which either could be executed, or would be consistent with liberty and justice. But though the law cannot hinder people of the same trade from sometimes assembling together, it ought to do nothing to facilitate such assemblies; much less to render them necessary (Smith p.129).

Adam Smith was absolutely right that the way to prevent people from figuring out how to "raise prices" was to keep them apart. That is also the first point I want to make about how people learn these forbidden lessons. They are collected from the experience of many people. This knowledge is social and collective. No one knows the whole thing, partly because it's always being renewed as situations change. Workers learn it by talking to each other, sharing stories, listening to each other, arguing, comparing, planning and critiquing. It is not a matter of individual smartness or good study habits.

Smith then lists three mistakes made by local governments that encourage or allow workers to assemble, get to know each other and conspire "against the publick." First, requiring tradesmen to register themselves "connects individuals who might never otherwise be known to one another." Taxing a trade to provide for their poor "gives them a common interest." Worst of all, allowing them to "incorporate" – that is, form a union – would be most foolish of all. You don't want workers to have job security. Having a union would have the effect on workers of alleviating "the fear of losing [their] employment which restrains his frauds and corrects his negligence" (p. 129).

Since Adam Smith, the means have changed, but not the ends.

No Posters about Rights

There was an article by Stephen Greenhouse in the *New York Times* (Saturday, April 14, 2012, on page B7: "Employers Don't Have to Post Union Notices, Judge Rules"):

> A federal judge in South Carolina ruled on Friday that the National Labor Relations Board did not have the authority to order most private employers to post notices telling workers about their right to unionize under federal law (Greenhouse, 2012, B7)

The lawsuit was filed by the US Chamber of Commerce against a requirement issued by the National Labor Relations Board (NLRB), the federal agency that oversees the administration and enforcement of the National Labor Relations Act (NLRA) of 1935. The requirement was that private sector employers should have to put up posters informing workers of their right to form unions and bargain collectively under the NLRA. According to Greenhouse, the NLRB argued that "many workers are unaware of their rights under the National Labor Relations Act," especially high school students, recent immigrants and workers in nonunion workplaces generally. Many federal and state agencies require notices to be posted in the workplace about everything from minimum wage to rest breaks to hand-washing. Most familiar are the OSHA (Occupational Health and Safety Act) 300-A posters that tell what toxics and hazards are present in a workplace. But up until 2011, the NLRB had not required comparable postings. The new leadership of the NLRB, appointed by the Democratic Obama administration, announced this requirement.

The decision of the court (the US Court of Appeals for the Fourth Circuit) was simply that the NLRB did not have the right to make a rule like that, one that required employers to inform workers of their rights (chttp://www.ca4.uscourts.gov/opinions/Published/121757.p.pdf). The issue, in other words, was framed not as what was reasonable for workers but what was allowed for the Board.

Putting this as simply as possible: the right to organize a union and bargain collectively has been federal law for private sector workplaces since 1935. The National Labor Relations Act was part of Roosevelt's New Deal. Many people do not know they have this right. Information about this right is apparently so sensitive that the Chamber of Commerce thinks it is worth filing a lawsuit to prevent its becoming more widely known. Not only that, but a judge (a Republican appointee) apparently agrees. In a previous case in a different federal court district, a different judge (a Democratic appointee) differed, saying "The notice-posting rule is a reasonable means of promoting awareness" (Greenhouse, *New York Times* p. B7, April 14, 2012).

Providing information about unions to workers in a workplace is always hard. Unions have to negotiate the right to set up a union bulletin board when members meet to develop and agree on a contract with their employers. Some employers deny this request. If the union gets permission to have a bulletin board, they have to negotiate what may be posted on it. If there is a general workplace announcement board and the employer allows charity food drive announcements or the like to be posted, then the union can also post announcements. But the dissemination of information coming from the union is tightly controlled. In practice, workers have to assume that information about their right to organize can be passed around only in the break room during break time or outside the gates of the workplace. Some employers forbid talking among workers at all. In one workplace I know, workers who were forbidden to talk started to sing; when they were forbidden to sing, they whistled.

Misinformation

The Greenhouse article happened to get printed the same week that Andrew Breitbart died. He was someone who made a living out of sensational misinformation. Misinformation is worse than no information; it takes up the space that information should occupy.

The Sunday *Times* of April 15, 2012 had a full-page article about him, chronicling his personal history as a right-wing agitator and provocateur, someone who seemed to have been born to use the internet's power to take a well-pitched story and create a crashing wave of viral interest, usually by some kind of fakery. The article listed several of his more famous stunts. In one, he took a quote from Shirley Sherrod, Director for Rural Development for the US Department of Agriculture in Georgia, out of context, leading to her dismissal from her job. She was later offered her job back, after apologies by President Obama. Another time he used an assistant, dressed up as a pimp, accompanied by another assistant dressed as a prostitute, to bait an employee at the community-based organization ACORN into what looked like illegal activity. The victim of this recently won a judgment against Breitbart's assistant in court.

One stunt attacked a labor education program like the one I taught in. The University of Missouri-Kansas City and the University of Missouri-St. Louis offered a labor education class called "Labor, Politics and Society" through a video network. A student in this class copied video recordings of the class available for student use only and gave them to Breitbart's editors. Breitbart's editors chopped up the video and reassembled it. One part showed one of the instructors saying, ""Violence is a tactic and it's to be used when appropriate." In fact, this was a quote from a documentary film about the 1968 Memphis Sanitation Workers strike and Martin Luther King's assassination. In the film, a young militant was questioning non-violence. Breitbart edited it the recording to make it sound as if the words had been spoken by the instructor. He put it and other edited clips up on his website, BigGoverment.com, and called the instructors "radical advocates of violence, sabotage and communism." He accused the University of Missouri of being a haven for Marxists.

Crying "Marxist!" even sixty or more years after Senator McCarthy used his bully pulpit to chase down supposed Communists still sets off sirens. But several of Brietbart's other stunts had been exposed as frauds by this time, so the mainstream media kept its cool until the labor educator, Judy Ancel, provided a response. What is unusual is that the administration of UMKC did not join the attack, but instead came out in support of Ancel. But Ancel's colleague in the class, a business manager of a large Operating Engineers local in St. Louis, did get fired both from his university job and his union job. He was later re-hired by the university after a campaign waged by labor educators through the United Association for Labor Education (UALE), faculty and students.

What links these stories together is this: they help answer the question, how is it possible that people are still asking, "Can they do that?"

In most states, when people go in to take the test for a driver's license, they get a booklet that explains the rules of the road. No such booklet accompanies job applications.

Labor Studies: State legislation to encourage or require it

These days, many high school students work, if not during the school year then through the summer. This was not always the case. More and more students got jobs in the 1980s due to the decline in real wages and the increasing need for sources of family income. One might expect that a focal point of their school curriculum would be the social relations of work: who can do what to whom, what the legal framework of it all is, how some things have improved and some haven't and what can be done about it. No teenager should graduate from high school without being able to answer the question, "Can they do that?" But they can't. Only a few states have passed laws saying that labor, labor history or labor studies should be included in the regular curriculum. These include Illinois, Iowa, Wisconsin, West Virginia, and California.

Illinois has a law requiring the teaching of labor history

in the schools, but it is unfunded and unimplemented. Wisconsin's 2009 law required the incorporation of the "history of organized labor in America and the collective bargaining process" into the state standards for social studies and convened a task force to plan implementation. However, this incorporation is planned to take place after standards for the overall social science curriculum have been completed. In the meantime, Wisconsin elected an extreme right-wing governor, who initiated a campaign against unions, including passing a law stripping public sector unions of many bargaining rights. The West Virginia legislature passed a resolution in 2010 establishing Labor History Week, which is supposed to follow Labor Day, the first Monday in September. However, the resolution adds, ".....the observance of Labor History Week is not intended to create a burden, financial or otherwise, for public schools, teachers or state institutions of higher education." The University of West Virginia Labor Center has developed curricula and works with schools to teach these sessions.

California has the most statutes requiring the study of labor. The Education Code requires grades 7 through 12 social sciences to include "the role of the entrepreneur and labor." The first week of April has been "Labor History Week" since 2002, and schools are supposed to "make pupils aware of the role the labor movement has played." Cesar Chavez Day has been March 31 since 2002 and every grade, Kindergarten through grade 12, is supposed to incorporate curriculum on Chavez and the history of the farm labor movement in California and the nation. There are also a number of History and Social Science Content Standards relating to labor, the most significant of which is for grade 11, when US history is taught. This standard requires classes to "evaluate the advances and retreats of organized labor, from the creation of the AFL and CIO to current issues of a post-industrial multinational economy, including the United Farm Workers in California."

There is a big difference, however, between having a law to encourage teaching labor studies and making it actually happen. Availability of curriculum is not the problem. California has a complete curriculum designed for high school students, created with the support of the California Federation of Teachers. The website of the American Labor Studies Foundation in Troy, New York, lists many kinds of curricula. Labor Education programs have numerous samples of curricula ready to go. A website called *Build the Wheel* at www.buildthe wheel.org collects and offers social justice curricula of all kinds. Nor is there a lack of volunteers; at Central Labor Council meetings in the Midwest, retired building trades union representatives bewail the ignorance of high school kids about labor and offer to go to schools and do presentations. In those states where a public interest in teaching labor in the schools has led to legislation, the barriers are not lack of curricula or lack of willing presenters. The barriers are the crowded, test-driven schedules of the school programs and the reluctance of school leaders to open up the politically tricky topic of the social relations of work among kids who are going out into their first jobs.

Attacks on Labor Research

In 1997, Representative Lane Evans (D-Illinois) introduced the Federal Procurement and Assistance Integrity Act (HR 1624), which would give the labor secretary the authority to debar or suspend companies from receiving federal contracts if they had a clear pattern or practice of violations of the National Labor Relations Act, the Occupational Safety and Health Act, or the Fair Labor Standards Act. This may not seem like a radical idea.

However, passing HR1624 would depend on public pressure on Congress, and public pressure depends on public information. Companies that violate labor laws will go to great lengths to prevent publicity about their bad labor practices.

Four days after the introduction of HR1624 there was a Congressional Town Meeting called by the same Representative Evans and other representatives to investigate the employment practices of Beverly Enterprises, a company that runs a 750-site chain of nursing homes. The National Labor Relations Board (NLRB) had charged this chain with committing some 135 unfair labor practices (UFLs) at 32 facilities in 12 states between mid-1986 and mid-1988, plus many more since then. A recent NLRB decision stated that "wide-ranging and persistent misconduct, demonstrat[ed] a general disregard for the employees' fundamental rights."

One of the expert witnesses at the Congressional Town Meeting was Kate Bronfenbrenner, a labor researcher at Cornell University. In the course of researching Beverly's labor relations practices, Bronfenbrenner had interviewed many employees and uncovered the reality behind the hundreds of violations of labor law.

Beverly Enterprises sued Bronfenbrenner, not for her actual testimony in front of the Town Meeting, which was protected speech, but for her reference to that testimony in a National Public Radio interview. They sued her for defamation and demanded both compensatory and punitive damages. Beverly's lawyers also demanded that she produce all the documents related to her research. This would have meant copying thousands of documents and would have revealed the names of many individual workers who had been promised confidentiality.

Eventually, Beverly dropped its lawsuit.

Ellen Dannin, the originator of a petition in defense of Bronfenbrenner and Professor at Penn State Dickinson School of Law, provided this interpretation of the attack:

The message was clear: corporations would fight back against attempts to report their bad labor practices in the media. The tactic of demanding copies of documents, including responses to surveys and all Bronfenbrenner's organizing research generally, was going to be typical of other attacks. The company hoped that the demand would be so burdensome that it would bring the work of the researcher, or the program, to a halt. It also clearly hoped that the administration of the university would be intimidated into cooperating with the demands of the attacker.

Cornell University, in fact, did fail to come to Bronfenbrenner's defense. Her own university was willing to cooperate with her attacker until pressure from colleagues at other universities and the labor movement persuaded the university otherwise.

The idea that labor law violators should be barred from getting federal contracts is still around. A congressional report issued some 15 years later by Democratic senators on the Health, Education, Labor and Pension Committee stated:

> Overall, the 49 federal contractors responsible for large violations of federal labor laws were cited for 1,776 separate violations of these laws and paid $196 million in penalties and assessments. In fiscal year 2012, these same companies were awarded $81 billion in taxpayer dollars. (Greenhouse, S. *New York Times*, p B1,B2, 12.11.2013)

The *New York Times* article in which this was covered focused on the billions of dollars in federal contracts awarded to these companies despite their records of wage theft, safety violations and worker fatalities.

Wall Street Journal and the Landmark Foundation

Many other college or university-based labor education programs have also been directly attacked. In August 2003 an opinion piece in the *Wall Street Journal* by Steve Malanga accused labor education programs generally of "supporting labor and its organizing efforts rather than educating students."

> Just when you thought our universities -- with their multi-culti [sic] curricula, anti-Americanism and intolerance of debate -- couldn't possibly get any more partisan, along comes the next new thing: the labor movement's successful co-opting of academic departments and programs (Malanga, 2003).

This came at a time when the Governor of California, Arnold Schwarzenegger, had twice eliminated the entire budget for the labor education and research centers in the University of California system, only to be overruled by the legislature.

Nationally, between 2005 and 2009 an organization called the Landmark Legal Foundation appeared to be going systematically from one labor education program to another with the complaint that public funds were being used to provide services for a "private interest," that is, labor unions.

The tactic, as in the Bronfenbrenner case, was often to try to drive a wedge between the program and the administration of the college or university. The demand for copies of documents was usually the first step in the attack. Most of the eleven programs which reported attacks to the United Association for Labor Education found that the demands faded away after the "wedge" tactic failed and university legal department or the Board of Regents sent a letter defending the labor program. The programs that received demands from Landmark and were able to repel them by turning the problem over to the legal or administrative structure were Florida International University, Indiana University, UCLA, UC Berkeley, University of Connecticut (this program has closed as of 2014), University of Iowa, University of Massachusetts at Amherst, University of Michigan, University of Minnesota, and the University of Wisconsin School for Workers.

Landmark could also be discouraged by being told they would be charged for photocopying. Twice, Landmark paid for photocopied materials; after that, the cost of photocopying seemed to put a stop to the demands.

Unfortunately, in one case, the challenge by Landmark succeeded in doing damage to a labor education program. This was at Evergreen State College in Washington State. Given Evergreen's liberal reputation, this might strike some as odd, but there is a difference between being generally in favor of social justice and being specifically in favor of worker's rights.

At Evergreen, Landmark's suggestion that the labor education program be audited went to both the state auditor, Brian Sonntag, and the college's own administration. The state auditor said an audit was not necessary, but stood aside. Then the college, instead of pushing back against Landmark's claim that the Labor Center was violating state law by working with labor unions, performed its own audit.

The college's internal auditor found that by providing education to unions the labor center was serving a "private interest" and that this should not be supported by public money (Kardas, 2012). In turn, the Labor Center responded with documentation about how the auditor had blatantly misread state law. Significant support came to the Center from the American Association of University Professors,

Evergreen's faculty union, and the Evergreen faculty as a whole.

Nevertheless, the Center's budget was cut in half, with no guarantees that it would not be further reduced or eliminated in the future. To save the Center and to provide it with a more secure home, the staff and the Center's advisory council worked with the state labor council to have the program moved to South Seattle Community College. There the program is thriving.

The closing of the National Labor College

As I write this, in December 2013, I have received news that the National Labor College, a small non-profit college in Silver Spring, Maryland, sponsored and subsidized by the American Federation of Labor-Congress of Industrial Organizations (AFL-CIO) to the tune of five to seven million dollars a year, is shutting down for good. This institution, which grew out of the George Meany Center, started by doing short-term union training programs, eventually offered a BA, and then added MA programs. While there is plenty of blame to go around on this one, the loss of this unique labor-centered institution hurts.

I have been teaching a class at the National Labor College for the past year, since I retired from the University of Illinois. I will miss these classes a lot. Any college-level social science or history class can learn about trade agreements, the recession, foreclosures and immigration policy. Regular college students are inevitably touched by these historic events. But they are touched as individuals. Those classes are not about how to do something collectively about them.

In a labor education class you move directly from learning about the Gini Index, a statistical measure of inequality, into an informed discussion of how people have made their own jobs better by organizing. Some talk about a specific abuse that got fixed. Others talk about organizing a union to begin with, negotiating a contract, winning a grievance, or more broadly raising the city minimum wage or supporting a winning candidate in a general election.

In labor education classes, we focus on the actions that link making work better for individuals and making work better for everyone. These discussions include ethical and political matters. Many of the students in the class will have experience in the fights that have been successful. It makes a huge difference to have students in a class who actually have experienced successes. It makes the enormous challenges we face less overwhelming.

Conspiring together

These scattered examples show how deep and broad the opposition to educating people about their rights at work actually is. This knowledge is not merely overlooked in schools. It is not missing because it is non-existent. It is missing because it is the target of a fight. Teaching about workers' rights is actually opposed, contested, distorted, corrupted with misinformation, blocked and forbidden.

Adam Smith was right; what is really dangerous is when people meet together and "conspire." The Latin roots of the word "conspire" actually mean "to hope or dream together."

So, what can education – not labor education, but mainstream education, the study of how people learn -- contribute to making these forbidden lessons better known and understood? We will explore this in the next chapter.

CHAPTER 4:
LABOR EDUCATION CLASSES: A PLACE TO CONSPIRE

Alone, you can fight,
you can refuse,
you can take what revenge you can,
but they roll over you...

But two people fighting back to back
can cut through a mob,
a snake-dancing file can break a cordon,
an army can meet an army.
— from *The Low Road*, by Marge Piercy

Labor education programs hold classes in which people intentionally, directly teach and learn how to take advantage of their rights at work and improve and protect their jobs and the jobs of others. In these classes, they talk and listen to each other. That is, they conspire.

Here is another brief story from one of my classes, just to show how this happens.

There were two women in this class who had never met before. One woman, Christine, worked in an office in a large hospital owned by a university. She had a son who had just graduated from high school. The son got into college and wanted to go. But because he didn't receive enough financial aid, the woman took a second job working in the warehouse of a publishing company packing books.

The jobs were very different. One was sedentary, sitting at a computer all day, while the other was physical, lifting and packing books into shipping boxes. Luckily, the jobs were near to each other, so she didn't have to go home in between. In fact, both the hospital and the publishing house were

33

owned by the same university.

Things went along well for a while. Over time, however, the woman, who was working eight to four-thirty and then five to midnight, became exhausted. In her day job she relied on the fact that her desk was off in a corner to allow her to take brief naps when things were slow.

One day her supervisor saw her sleeping and fired her. When the woman tried to explain why she was so tired, she unintentionally revealed that she was working a second job. The supervisor at her first job called up the supervisor at her other job, and she was fired from that job, too. Then she had no job at all.

Christine told her story in class. The other woman, named Millie, heard Christine's story and said she knew of a similar situation. It also involved a woman who had worked two jobs. These were custodian jobs in big high-rise office buildings downtown. These jobs take place at night. The women who clean the offices and bathrooms in these buildings walk in while the office workers are walking out.

The woman Millie was talking about would work from five to midnight at one job, and then cross the street and work from midnight to five at another job. Then she would go home, pack lunches for her kids and husband, wake them up, feed them breakfast and get them off to school, and go to bed. She would sleep from eight to two, get up and do the housework and shopping, pick up the kids, make their dinner and leave for work and work all night.

Somehow in this case, too, the supervisor found out that the woman was working two jobs and fired her. Again, it turned out that both buildings were under contract with the same custodial company. In other words, the woman had the same employer at both jobs. This woman was working twelve hours a day, five days a week, or sixty hours a week.

The woman who was fired did not know if she had any rights at all in this situation. However, she was desperate, so she contacted Millie, who was her union representative. When Millie realized that this woman was putting in twenty hours of overtime every week she knew that this woman should have been paid time and a half for each one of those twenty extra hours. With this information, they went to the employer and the woman got a settlement of almost $2,000 ($140 per week going back twelve weeks). She also got her job back, although only one of them.

There is a lot more going on in these stories than just what Millie knew compared to what Millie's member or Christine knew. It's not just about information, although that was crucial. The difference is actually access to a whole set of living resources that enables someone to act strategically in a critical moment. Such a moment occurs when there is a balance of power that can tilt one way or the other. At a moment like that, what you add to one end of the scale or the other can make all the difference. This moment itself is a complex product of conditions, constraints, opportunities and talents.

In order to make the balance of power tilt your way, you have to be able to work with the whole set of living resources, which means looking at the big picture. The knowledge that matters is more than facts. "What should we do?" and "With whom should we do it?" and "What order should we do it in?" are just as important as "What do we know?"

Through hearing these stories, the other students in the class got a quick overview of that big picture. It included how burdensome college costs have become; how adult children are relying so much on their parents these days; how little someone earns, even when doing heavy physical work; how complex the levels of subcontracting are in the business services industry, and how much parents are willing to spend down their energy and health in order to see the next generation go to the college they want or get off to school on time in the morning. In the background of these two stories we can see the outline of an economy that requires the older generation to make extreme sacrifices as they try to lift the next generation up into the shrinking middle class. It also gives us a look at how workplaces themselves have become sterner and less forgiving as employers look for ways to stay in business and make whatever money they can, in the expectation that things are only going to get worse, not better.

These trends are known to most people, of course, but it takes a specific concrete case to bring home what it is like for the people who are living through it. Listening to Christine tell her story first, hearing her voice and seeing her expression and body language, teaches us how confusing and terrifying it is to lose a job. Then listening to Millie, who has a good union staff job to back her up, and hearing her voice and seeing her expression as she tells about going to management and making them pay her member the money that was owed her – those were both lessons in the realities of life and the forms that courage takes. The other people in the class could watch, listen and think: "This is what someone looks like when they are afraid; this is what someone looks like when they win." Then the question is, can we help the frightened person win, too? They could see the whole picture as a backdrop behind their two classmates.

Christine actually did get her job back. She got it back herself. Her union did not offer to help. Her conversation with Millie, who worked for a different union, gave her the knowledge that she did have rights. The other students in the class gave her confidence to go back to her boss and plead her case. She went to management and begged, and they gave her another chance. I do not know what happened to her son.

The messiness of this story demonstrates how learning the forbidden lessons about rights on the job comes out of a shared experience. Sometimes the exchange of experience and information occurs within the union structure. Other times it comes through attending labor education classes. And sometimes it comes when workers meet off the job, on their own, and break bread and shed tears together.

Now we will look at four ways of understanding how this exchange of experience happens and why it produces learning.

CHAPTER 5:
FOUR LEARNING THEORIES

I believe we should examine the kinds of learning and thinking in action that we need to develop – the kinds of reflective practitioner we need to be – in the face of evil people and inimical forces, in front of the earth movers about to knock down a forest, in front of the lines of people with guns, in conflict with union busters, in confrontation with the snobs and belittlers, the despoilers and the polluters - that is, in the presence of enemies.
— Michael Newman, *Defining the Enemy: Adult Education in Social Action*, p. 54

First, what is a theory?

A theory is an idea that relates things to each other. If you think of these things as cities, mountains, roads and rivers in a landscape, a theory is the map and the compass that will get you around. The theory explains where things are in relation to each other.

Theories never exist by themselves. Where there is one theory, you will find other theories, other paths or routes.

Theories also have histories, because they develop over time to explain new things that come along. Theories don't come out of nowhere; they are created through debate and discussion. People become friends or lifelong enemies depending on how they feel about certain theories. Theories that cover a lot of issues are sometimes called "world views."

When scholars use a theory, they use it because it is known to many people in their field and can serve as a common frame of reference with terms that are familiar even if the specific application is unfamiliar. This book is an example of that. I am using theories that are familiar to people in the field of education in the hope that I can get them to focus on the realities of learning at work that separates education and labor. In the reverse direction, I am describing what happens in labor education classes in the hope that I can show labor people how to use what education has to offer education. Better yet would be to knock the wall down.

Theories of learning

The soul: Two hundred years ago the study of learning was part of theology. The discourse of learning was all about the soul, the spirit, the heart.

The mind: By the late 19th century, as religion began to lose its all-encompassing control of scholarship, German philosophers, including Marx, Hegel and Wilhelm Wundt, were talking in terms of the mind instead of the soul. The way you would study the mind would be through introspection. Freud's method, psychoanalysis, was a way of studying the mind by introspection. Wundt actually started doing experiments and set up one of the first psychology labs.

Consciousness: The word "consciousness" came to stand for what the mind did, meaning a state of being awake and aware, alert to one's own place in the world and the relations of others to you and to each other.

Behavior: After World War I, the study of learning shifted toward what could be observed from the outside. In the United States, this was called Behaviorism. Behaviorists studied how people – or rats, for that matter – responded to stimuli, rewards and punishments.

The Brain: When Behaviorism in the United States eventually connected with computer science, people started talking about the brain instead of the mind, much less the soul.

Cognition: Today, although learning theory in the United States has embraced much of what has emerged elsewhere, learning theory is often called "cognitive science," which reveals its historical roots in Behaviorism, artificial intelligence and computer sciences.

In Eastern Europe, and especially in the Soviet Union, another trend was developing that stayed parallel with Behaviorism in the United States for a while but then diverged. The Russian Revolution had taken place and for a few years Moscow was a center of tremendous intellectual and creative energy. The overarching framework was the Marxist analysis of how societies work. A central concept of Marxism is dialectics, the back-and-forth movement of forces in a historical process of change and development. "Consciousness" in this framework is not just about one's own place in the social world, but is itself shaped by the social world.

Two theorists emerged out of this second trend. These are L.S. Vygotsky (1896-1934) and Paulo Freire (1921-1997). The works of these two men, who never met and who came from different sides of the world, form the backdrop for most contemporary theories that think it is important to consider the social context of learning: Who is learning, where are they learning, and why are they learning?

At the core of their work is the idea that human beings are shaped by the social worlds around them and have the power to shape those worlds in return. In other words, a person learns a certain way because of how they relate to the world and the social relationships around them. This is basically different from saying that a person learns a certain way because they are smart, or because they were born gifted or stupid. It is also different from thinking of the brain as a computer that can be fed information.

Obviously, if you want to teach people, the theory you choose to shape your teaching makes a big difference. If you design a school system or a class based on the idea that some people are born smart and some people are born stupid, or that individual willpower and attitude are all it takes, it will look very different from a school system or class based on the idea that people learn by doing things, working with other people, and talking about what they think.

Because some of these people for whom I am writing this book are teachers, I want to say a few words about Vygotsky and Freire. Many teachers already know something about them. Their work provides the backdrop for the theories which I will explain in the pages that follow.

Vygotsky

The brilliant young man who was at the center of the intellectual ferment in Moscow following the Russian Revolution was named Lev Semyenovich Vygotsky. He died at the age of 38, of tuberculosis, leaving a network of colleagues and students and a few important influential works. The first to appear in the US, in 1961, was *Thought and Language.*

Language in learning: Vygotsky focused on the role of language, which has its origins in the social world. The meanings of words, phrases and even longer units of language like songs are continuously re-negotiated in order to carry meaning between and among people. "Is this what you mean?" someone might ask. "Or do you mean something else?" Talking or otherwise communicating with each other changes people's consciousness. It makes learning possible. Language is like a stepping stone between what is inside our heads and what is outside, The term for what language does in Vygotsky's theory is 'mediate'. Changes in people's thinking, from babyhood to adulthood, come not only from physical growth but are mediated through communications with others.

Learning with others: One of his best-known ideas, often used by teachers, is called the "zone of proximal development," which says that if a person works closely with a more expert peer or colleague, they become able to do things that they would not be able to do by themselves. Examples of things that they might do would be, solve a puzzle, develop a strategy, or figure out a good explanation. This helping hand is not like cheating; in fact, it makes real learning more rapid. If learning is really social, we should also ask: Are we smarter together? And if we are, what does that say about "being smart"?

Vygotsky's work was suppressed by the Soviet dictator Stalin but was carried on by Vygotsky's friends and colleagues. To speak about his ideas safely, they often had to attribute them to Pavlov, the psychologist who trained dogs to salivate when he rang a bell and whose name is associated with "conditioned response." Pavlov had Stalin's approval, so it was safe to talk about Pavlov's ideas.

Ironically, when Vygotsky's ideas finally came to the United States in the 1960s, they came in part because the Soviet Union was now a powerhouse. The United States government was both afraid of socialism and eager to understand "the new Soviet man," in case a new kind of human personality had been born under socialism. By the time Vygotsky's ideas were studied in the United States, they had spread around the world. They were shaping the education policies of countries just coming out of colonialism in Central America and Africa.

Freire

The other important theorist who focused on learning in a social context is Paolo Freire, the Brazilian educator. He is best known for his work teaching groups of landless peasants in Brazil how to read and then how to use their new literacy to claim the political rights they needed to survive. He would go to a remote village, sit with the villagers and ask them to tell him about what was important in their lives.

The answers were likely to be "the well," "the house," "the cows and pigs," "the children." Freire would start with these words and show the villages how to write them down. Then, by using the sounds of the syllables from those words, he would build up a vocabulary of other words that would soon become large enough to be used for written communication. Legend has it that he was able to bring literacy to a village in three weeks.

His work inspired a national network of study centers to build literacy. After a military coup in 1964 he was imprisoned and then went into exile. Linking learning and power can be risky.

In *The Pedagogy of the Oppressed* (1968) he wrote vividly and convincingly about the experience of poverty and illiteracy. The Portuguese term that people associate with Freire's work is *conscientização*, which translates more or less as "consciousness-raising" or "critical consciousness." This is knowledge that has depth, emotional potency, and political perspective, and is shared or collective. It is essentially the same as the kind of knowledge developed by and for dealing with the challenges of a bad job. I mentioned earlier that another word we could use for consciousness is "readiness," in the sense of the state of being aware, conscious, prepared, equipped, in touch with others and ready to fight if necessary.

Anyone who works with the extremely poor can learn by studying Freire. Freire's theories, widely known as "popular education," became the framework for literacy campaigns in countries undergoing revolutions, like Cuba and Nicaragua, where the new leaders needed to bring up the education level of whole populations very quickly.

You might ask why learning theories developed in countries undergoing revolutions are useful in the US today.

Vygotsky was doing his most important work during the chaotic period after the Russian Revolution, when many people expected to build a new kind of society. Freire's theories developed in Brazil at a time of extreme inequality. These theories, with their focus on the social context of learning, were also theories of social change, strategies to support movements for social justice.

There are lots of theories of social change, what it is and why and how it happens. However, a theory of learning is only a theory of social change if it explains how the learning of individuals is also the learning of a whole group of people, and how they collectively improve or even save their lives. If a theory of learning only explains how one individual can hop up the ladder of opportunity, leaving the rest behind and the rungs of the ladder unchanged, that is not a theory of learning and social change.

In the US, we are not actually all that far from being in the same situation as Brazil and Russia when these theories were being developed. The Washington Post Worldview reported on January 31, 2014, that the US ranks 44th out of 88 industrialized countries in inequality, just above Russia today and Turkey. We have a large and growing population of the "extremely poor" that includes not just people who are unemployed and looking for jobs, but millions of low-wage workers. These are people who cannot live on what they earn even when working two or three jobs. In fact, a spring 2012 report from the Organization for Cooperation and Economic Development (OCED) said that the United States has the highest percent of low-wage workers of any industrialized country. These are working people who are unhappy about what their wages can buy them in our economy where so many essential doors to opportunity, like education, are barred by high pay-walls.

So what might be the most appropriate set of learning theories for a country like ours today? One that measures how smart people are and rewards them for who they are, or one that offers a way for people to work together and improve life for everyone? This question happens to be at the heart of the current struggle over the future of education.

Obviously, labor education is going to draw from a set of theories that can support a social justice strategy. As we will see in Chapter 13, when we talk about teachers organizing to control the conditions and contexts of their work, there are some powerful forces lined up on the other side, the side that prefers to sort and track people on the basis of their individual qualities and accomplishments. Sorting and tracking help individuals climb the ladders of opportunity but do not change where the rungs are or increase the number of ladders.

We are now going to talk about four specific theories of learning that can be used to understand complex situations involving power and collective action. They are in the overall tradition of Vygotsky and Freire because they focus on social context and collective learning. If you want to learn more about the overall tradition that these theories come from, search for them using the term Cultural-Historical Activity Theory, or CHAT.

Four learning theories

The theories we are going to look at are:

- *Kolb's learning cycle,* which models the step-by-step process by which people first experience an event, then learn from it;
- *Communities of practice,* which explains how people share what they know and pass it from one generation to another;
- *Work process theory,* which focuses on people solving problems collectively, in networks;
- *Activity Theory,* which explains the politics of workplace learning and distinguishes between what the employer wants to teach and what the worker needs to learn. This

theory also helps us see where conflict is likely to arise and why learning carries so much emotion.

In the chapters that follow this one, I will give case studies of situations at work where a great deal of learning of different kinds was going on. No one theory will explain everything in these chapters, which are all from real life. But using the theories together, we can separate out the learning from some of the other things that are going on, and pay it some respect. We can also see what went well, what went wrong, and what was learned.

After explaining the four useful theories I will offer you a dangerous theory that I call the *Tarzan theory*. The *Tarzan theory* says that learning is the result of being born smart and having a good attitude and willpower. Many of us have been taught in schools designed according to the *Tarzan theory*. What is amazing is that we learned anything at all.

Kolb's Learning Cycle

The first theory is known as *Kolb's Learning Cycle* (See Diagram 1 p. 48). Daniel Kolb was an educator at the University of Chicago in the 1980's who made the argument that learning is a process. This process has steps. First this happens, then that, then something else. So what are the steps in learning? Kolb drew a circle, and marked the different steps around the circle going clockwise from midnight (see pg. 48).

Kolb published his most famous paper in 1984, and people have been referring to it ever since. There are many versions of the learning cycle image on the internet. They use different terms for each step in the process. The first step is always called something like *experiencing*. This is a concrete experience or an event. It means that something happens to a person. Perhaps it's a crisis, a trauma, or an illness. It could also be winning a contest or an election, taking a class or

Diagram 1. Kolb's Learning Cycle

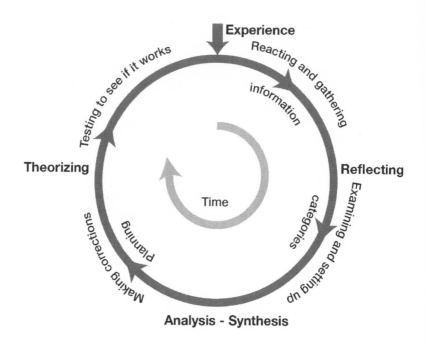

reading something. The main idea is that something happens to you, whether you initiated it yourself or whether it came from somewhere else.

The second step is *reflection*: thinking about something, mulling it over, organizing your thoughts, tossing them around in conversation, de-briefing. This step is sometimes called *categorizing* because your world has been disturbed by the event, and now you are gathering your thoughts together and grouping them in categories. In this step, you need information. Here is where you will draw on your background knowledge as you decide what to call something, what it looks like, what other examples of it are. You may do some research or at least ask questions. For example, the worker with the mop in Chapter 2 might want to know what his contract says (if he has one). Or he might go and look in the locker where the mops are kept to see if there are other tools for dealing with a spill. He hasn't decided what to do yet because he is still sorting things out.

In the third step, which this theory calls *abstracting*, you are putting the pieces of the experience back together into something that makes sense to you – a relationship of some sort. The worker with the mop remembers that the burns on another worker's arms are from acid, and that when that worker shouted out in pain the supervisor just told him to go wash down at the sink and get back to work. This reminds him that another worker stepped forward at that moment and demanded that the worker with the burns see a doctor. There are people he can trust to give him advice, in other words. Another word for this is "synthesis," a word with Greek roots that means "putting things together," from the word "syn" which means "together" and "tithenai," to put in a place.

The fourth step is the one in which you *test* what you have figured out in step three. You have made sense of the experience and have decided what has to happen next. You *experiment*. You could also say that at this point, you are forming a theory of the experience. You see if the theory works. For the worker who has been told to clean up the spill, this might mean putting down the mop and going to look for his co-worker who had stepped forward previously.

Going through these steps takes time. An emergency room nurse told me that in her training she should expect that 20% of her learning would take place while she is working on the patient and 80% would take place afterwards when she was thinking about it and talking about it. That gives us an idea of the proportion of time that we should expect to spend on each step of the cycle. The experience itself, the first step, is one fifth of the process of learning.

Kolb's Learning Cycle is important because it makes clear

how much learning depends on taking the time to think about something. People are not photocopy machines. You can't hold a piece of paper with writing on it in front of someone and claim that you've taught them something. You can't show someone a set of Power Point slides and expect learning to have taken place, even if you "cover everything." Learning begins with an experience, but then that experience has to be digested. The different steps are what happen in the digestion process. Information is most important in the second step, when you're sorting out what happened. After that, what matters is thinking and talking with other people. That requires time, opportunities to discuss things with others, the freedom to criticize or re-frame, and sometimes permission to mention a wild idea.

When information is choked off and misinformation abounds, learning is hard enough. But the rest of the steps are equally important and equally easy to interfere with. Teachers often skip steps because they think that they have to cover the topic and get on to the next topic. People who have to learn on their own may be unable to find someone to talk with. They may have heard partial information in a moment of crisis and are afraid or angry and can't actually grasp what they are being told. They may be being fed lies. It takes good luck as well as time to work through the stages of *Kolb's Learning Cycle*.

There are limitations to Kolb's theory. For our purposes, it leaves out several important factors. To begin with, it seems to be about a single individual person learning alone. In real life, the second, third and fourth steps are best taken with other people, using conversation, debate and teamwork. *Kolb's learning cycle* doesn't give us a tool to link to the social context in which the learning is happening, and we're interested in that context. Social context is the essence of the *CHAT* (Cultural-historical activity theory) approach. In every workplace, regulations, laws, history, customs, practices, tools, resources, money, allies and enemies all matter. Therefore, a full theory of learning at work should take into account all of these.

Kolb also doesn't account for learning that takes place in a struggle, which is how much workplace learning takes place. The fact that trying to get control of your work involves a struggle means that what you learn will be full of emotions, including fear, anger and sometimes joy and relief. If the only theory we are using is *Kolb's learning cycle*, we might not be ready to meet the emotions that pile up in what people learn at work. We might think that a person can, for example, survive a near-miss industrial accident and then calmly sort out or analyze the experience and decide what to do. We know this doesn't happen. Labor union stewards who deal with workers who need help know this. The first flood of speech that comes out of the distressed worker's mouth is often incoherent and contradictory. The steward's first job is to let the words flow and wait until they can ease the person into the second step. But this is never simple or easy. Some employment situations, even though they don't involve physical risk, are so stressful that the crisis part of the learning cycle never shifts into the second step. When this happens, nothing is learned.

So there is a lot more to learning than just *Kolb's Learning Cycle*.

Communities of practice

The second theory about how people learn is this: we learn things not as information plus individual thinking, but as part of a *practice*. Practice is a term that has both a commonsense, vernacular meaning and meanings that are specific to philosophy (where it is closely related to *praxis*, the combination of action and theory). It also shows up in labor law, where we have the concept of "past practice," meaning something that has been done regularly in the past and has become accepted as a legitimate way of doing things.

The empirical research that produced this theory began with the question, "How does learning happen when there aren't any schools?" Since knowledge of various sorts has been passed from one generation to another for thousands of years without formal schools, this is an important question. The answer is that people can learn something *in practice* by doing it with other people. People learn by being among others who are doing something and participating in what they are doing.

The idea of a *community of practice* as a way of understanding how people learn was put forward in a small, influential book published in 1991 by Jean Lave, an anthropologist, and Etienne Wenger, titled *Situated Learning: Legitimate Peripheral Participation* (Cambridge University Press, 1991). Wenger was one of Lave's graduate students when she was a professor at U.C. Berkeley. The original problem that Lave was trying to explore was how people learned when they were not obviously being taught in a classroom. Lave adopted apprenticeships as a model for this teaching and learning, defining them broadly.

In *Situated Learning,* she and Wenger present five different cases of apprenticeships: people learning to sew clothing in a tailor shop in a marketplace in Liberia, people learning to be quartermasters (non-commissioned officers in charge of nautical charts) in the Navy, people learning to be meat cutters, people learning to participate in Alcoholics Anonymous, and people learning to be midwives in the Yucatan of Mexico. She abstracted from what these different situations had in common and proposed the term by which they could be described: A *community of practice.*

The tailors in Liberia work with their sewing machines in booths in the marketplace. A would-be tailor is not given direct instruction, as in a class. He doesn't learn by making a whole suit of clothes from start to finish. Instead, he joins in.

He learns a simple operation first and then moves on to other operations when the master tailor tells him to, contributing to the overall production. He has to learn not only how to operate the machine but also how to talk to the person who brings him the cloth and what the pecking order is for getting jobs. A young girl in the Yucatan whose grandmother is a midwife may start with tasks like running to bring the news of an oncoming birth, holding the lantern, or washing towels. What these learning experiences share is that the new student or novice learns how to be accepted by the rest of the workers or team as someone who will be learning their craft, recognized by the master or leader, and given useful work to do.

Some communities of practice in Lave and Wenger's research were more and some were less successful at bringing in new people as participants and teaching them how to do what the community did. These communities are complex contexts and have internal contradictions that can undermine their potential to survive. The continuity and survival of the community from one generation to the next depend on whether the community can develop new members and pass along the skills and expertise of the community. Therefore the ability to bring in new participants and bring them up to a level of expertise or leadership is critical. Without it, the community and the skills and expertise that characterize it, will die out.

Here are some of the features of a successful community of practice:

- Beginners must feel and believe that they are legitimate participants in the organization. For our purposes, this could be a workplace, a trade, a union, or a political organization. They must feel they have a right to be there. Their legitimacy must be confirmed by the leaders of the organization.
- The path from beginner to expert or leader must

be public, known or knowable to everyone, and transparent. There can't be any secret rules or hidden traps that someone who is trying to learn or get more involved can fall into. The transparency of the path from beginner to mature participant is itself a resource of the community of practice.

- The work that beginners do must be real work that contributes both to what other workers are trying to do (build a building, organize a campaign, run a union). It can't be make-work or busy work. It has to have "use value" and be something that is part of, or that will lead to, what a real expert does.

These are features of a successful *community of practice*, defined as a community that can survive the passage of time and pass on the skills that it nurtures from one generation of practitioners to the next. When we think about how a union may be suffering losses of membership and workplace power, we might evaluate it in terms of these three features. Is it doing what has to be done in order to survive into the next generation?

In Chapter 9 I will compare the experiences of third-year apprentices in the on-the-job training (OJT) phase of a formal union apprenticeship program with the experiences of graduates of a pre-apprenticeship program who are looking for work. Although the apprentices have to take initiative and earn the attention of the journeymen around them who are supposed to be helping them learn their trade, and although sometimes the journeymen are not good teachers, they still form a community of practice. The apprentices are supposed to be there. Everyone knows why they are there. They are connected to the journeymen and to the industry through a complex of economic agreements. Unless there is a serious violation of the norms of the community of practice, the apprentices will learn their trade, become journeymen themselves and train other apprentices.

Lave's work is highly influential in the world of education in the US. In the 1980's it became part of the overall swing in education as an academic discipline towards studying learning in context. Her early studies (1988) of how adults use math in everyday life revealed the difference between how they did on math tests and how they did when shopping for family groceries on a limited budget. This helped break down the wall between school learning and everyday learning. Her work shared much of the theoretical framework of Vygotskian and CHAT perspectives, which asserted the importance of viewing thinking and consciousness in its social context. Wenger himself went on to study communities of practice in business settings, while Lave continued (and continues) to work in the socio-cultural or CHAT tradition.

The *community of practice* perspective is specifically not about school learning, although one could try to design a school or even a classroom as a community of practice. But that is not what the idea is for. This perspective works best for asking the question, "Does this group of people have collective habits and norms that are strong enough to pass what they know and do on to another generation?"

Real communities of practice are fragile, even ephemeral things. They seem to develop in the absence or around the margins of strong institutional structures. Indeed, using the analytic perspective of a community of practice for designing learning is not a quick route to efficiency, economy or control. Yet over the history of our species communities of practice have carried most of the burden of passing survival knowledge on from one generation to another.

The community of practice perspective does not explain what happens in the face of direct conflict, such as when workers and employers confront each other over working conditions. In fact, the only kind of conflict that Lave and Wenger discuss in *Situated Learning* is intergenerational conflict; when the next generation has acquired enough expertise to rise to replace the older generation. What happens when a community of practice is threatened with suppression or has to carry on its developmental work while facing opposition or conflict? Answering *that* question requires another kind of theory. *Work Process Knowledge* theory shows how problems themselves can be the cause of the creation of knowledge.

Work Process Knowledge

The phrase "work process knowledge" is an English translation of the German word, *Arbeitsprozesswissen*, which was introduced by the German industrial psychologist Wilfried Kruse in 1986. In the 1980's, industries were just beginning to shift over to a high-tech, team-based work design that relied on computers and internet-based communications. The old-style workplace relationships, handed down from the traditions developed for assembly line production and known as "Fordist," did not match this new workplace. The new work design would require new social relationships of work. *Work Process Knowledge* was a way to formally recognize what people learn from actually doing the work in these high-tech workplaces. It was a way to encourage workers to get together to solve problems and then share what they learn throughout the workplace.

We are not as interested in problems about the technical challenges of production as we are in the social relationships of earning a living. For our purposes, we can use *Work Process Knowledge theory* to place problems of social relationships in stage center.

Nicholas Boreham, a professor at the University of Stirling in Scotland, conducted research for the European Union to gather descriptions of this transition. In 2002, with two other researchers, Martin Fischer and R. Samurçay, he produced a book that compiled reports from ten countries. Like Lave and

Wenger, they built their theories empirically from studies of different workplaces: air traffic control, a chemical plant, a computer-controlled machine tool shop, a debt collection call center, and others.

Work Process Knowledge values problems. If there are no problems, there is no learning. When a problem faces a worker, that worker has to exercise his knowledge of the whole system in order to start picking it apart. He has to know who else to bring in to help. He has to explain the problem to them. He has to look for a comparable situation elsewhere or in the past that might apply to this problem. If the solution to the problem draws on solutions to other problems, it will apply to even more other problems later. This means that the solution to the problem will have general value. It will have a theoretical dimension. The problem itself is what causes the creation of this knowledge.

When we look at someone learning through the lens of *Work Process Knowledge*, we will see them go through all the stages of *Kolb's Learning Cycle*, but the difference is that *Work Process Knowledge* assumes that the process is shared. It is collective (See Diagram 2. p. 58). No one individual worker possesses it all. Others bring what they know to the solution. Even the person who solves the problem knows only a part of the knowledge that is brought to the solution. The rest is shared throughout the organization itself.

By now you should be noticing that these theories, although they focus on different aspects of learning, work together well. They provide different ways of looking at the same thing.

Boreham wrote a paper in 2004 called "Collective Competence and Work Process Knowledge." He described *collective competence*. A group that has *collective competence* can face challenges and accomplish goals. They achieve collective competence by first talking about a situation and exchanging thoughts and feelings to collective sense of a situation. Second, they draw on the historical knowledge and experience of the group and its context. Third, the members of the group recognize their dependency on each other, "without which the members may act without regard for the collective purpose or each other's needs" (Boreham 2004, p. 4).

Diagram 2. Learning as Work Process

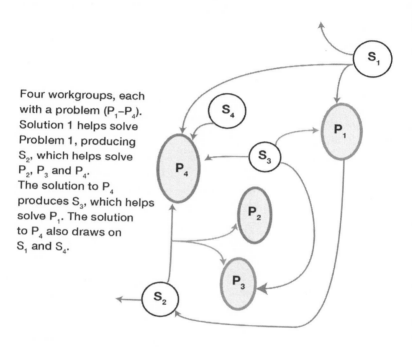

Four workgroups, each with a problem (P_1–P_4). Solution 1 helps solve Problem 1, producing S_2, which helps solve P_2, P_3 and P_4. The solution to P_4 produces S_3, which helps solve P_1. The solution to P_4 also draws on S_1 and S_4.

Work Process Knowledge or *collective competence* is created through problem-solving on the job in a way that is the opposite of the "waterfall" approach to organizing work. Traditionally, all manufacturing production was organized by this "waterfall" approach. In the "waterfall" approach, all planning is done ahead of time. All the knowledge belongs to the planners, who are management. The whole project is broken down into small parts. Once work starts, workers carry out their bit of the plan. There is no way for what they learn to circle back up to the original plan and adjust it to reflect the solutions to problems that have emerged while the work gets done. There is no way to learn from doing the work. Water only flows downhill, from planning to product. This means that if the planning has not correctly envisioned every tiny detail, which it never can, the whole project is at risk.

This is also a familiar state of affairs in top-down bureaucracies.

Frederick Winslow Taylor, the founder of "scientific management," believed that this knowledge could be stripped from the minds of workers and captured by management. In his view, workers were the hands, management was the brains. Management designed the waterfall, workers just rode the flow downhill. For Taylor, if workers knew more than the boss, he would say "the bosses' brains are under the worker's cap," and that was something to avoid.

The great innovation of the Toyota company was to change the way information flowed in manufacturing. Toyota's Kaizen system of "continuous improvement" encouraged workers to communicate what they were learning about problems on the line back up to management, so that mistakes in the plan could be changed. *Work Process Knowledge* theory goes beyond this: it not only has workers reporting problems, it has them solving them.

Note that Boreham, Fischer and Samurçay focus on production. *Work Process Knowledge* theory is intended to be useful in understanding how workers manage the complex processes of production in high-tech and knowledge-intensive workplaces, not on the challenges of earning a living in those contexts. This is interesting, because although what they are asking is how changes in technology and work process have impacted the social relationships of work, they do not look at whether the new social relationships of work have changed how people organize to earn a decent living.

No matter how low-tech or low-wage the workplace, such as a restaurant kitchen or a laundry facility in a hospital, the human relationships related to earning a living there will be complex. They will require constant innovation and the ability to respond quickly. We can draw on *Work Process Knowledge* theory to explain how people learn to manage and negotiate those relationships, no matter how high-tech the workplace is.

So what is *Work Process Knowledge*?

First, *Work Process Knowledge* is immediately useful for work. What you learn is relevant. This is like the "real work" that an apprentice is given in a community of practice, as part of the spiral path toward becoming an expert.

Second, *Work Process Knowledge* is theoretical, or at least includes a dimension of theoretical understanding. Workers learn as they make "efforts to resolve contradictions between what the theory predicts will happen (or what standard operating procedures are telling the workers to do) and the reality that confronts them" (Boreham 2002, 9). To resolve a problem – in human social relations as well as in the production of, for example, painted metal or electrical current – one must be able to generalize both about what is happening and what should be happening, which immediately leads one to thinking on a theoretical level.

Third, *Work Process Knowledge* is collectively held "not just throughout a workforce but in the very collective memory of communities of practice and artifacts and technology within them" (Boreham 2002, 9). It is triggered or stimulated by the work that a collective or a workforce is doing, it is matured by them and it belongs to them.

We can go back to the story of the man with the mop who has been told to clean up a spill. He has paused before going ahead with his task. He realizes that he doesn't know what to do. He goes and talks to some other workers about his problem. But what exactly is the problem? Is it: "If I refuse, will I get fired?" Or: "What kind of liquid is that on the floor?" Or: "Should I trust our supervisor to know what's safe?" The first problem is to identify the problem. The group, very likely, can respond to all these versions of the problem. One knows the contract and knows what will probably happen if he refuses the order. One knows what the liquid is. Maybe the man with the acid scars has a word to say about the supervisor. Meanwhile, the liquid is pooling under some machines. Something has to be done. Long-term, the leak has to be fixed, but short-term, the liquid has to be handled safely. They talk it over. Then they go as a group to the supervisor and explain the right way to handle the cleanup. If all goes well, the supervisor, faced with a group of workers, agrees and provides the proper equipment. The man with the mop has learned many things, the most important of which is what he can do with the help of his co-workers.

These three theories deal with learning as a process, learning as a community that has to pass its capabilities on to the next generation, and learning as problem-centered, collective and slightly theoretical. We now turn to the most complicated of theories of how people learn, *Activity Theory*.

Activity Theory and class conflict

Activity Theory is a current version, much elaborated, of the thinking of Alexei Leont'ev (1903 -1979) an associate of Vygotsky. Its most well-known current proponent is Yrjo Engeström at the University of Helsinki in Finland. For the purposes of studying learning in the workplace, *Activity Theory* is useful because it gives us a way to focus on purpose, allies and opposition, and see what changes occur when conflict causes a shift in the balance of power. In fact, it proposes that change and development (and learning *is* change and development) take place through the workings-out of disagreements and conflicts. This describes learning both on the level of small groups and on the level of society. Conflicts occur and resolve. The balance of power shifts. People look back on what has happened and talk about it. They figure out what to do and take the next steps. This sounds like *Kolb's Learning Cycle* because it is a process with steps. It also sounds like *Work Process Knowledge* because working through the problems is where the learning takes place, although the problems are problems in social relationships, not technical challenges.

However, there are three aspects of *Activity Theory* that make it valuable for understanding how people learn at work.

- *Activity Theory* tells us to keep our eyes on why people are doing something. Motivation is what matters.
- *Activity Theory* allows us to separate people who share our purpose (our friends) from people who don't. These other people may be intentionally trying to exploit us or may simply have a different agenda. Thus, activity theory is political.
- By recognizing the potential for conflict associated with change, we can appreciate how learning can be deeply emotional.

Activity Theory became mainstream in Europe post-World War II but not in the United States because postwar Europe developed with the political system called social democracy. Social democracies, as compared to our liberal democracy, accept the idea that there is fundamental conflict between social classes in all capitalist societies, but then build a social welfare state to undercut that conflict by reducing inequality. Social democracies also encourage labor unions, at least up to a point. Labor negotiations are seen as a regulated, civilized way to agree on working conditions despite fundamental conflicts of interest.   Therefore in Europe there is less theoretical resistance to the expectation of finding instances of class conflict in a given situation.

Activity theory has never become mainstream in the United States, where policy makers do not officially accept that class conflict is an inherent part of the social system. As a result, we do not have theories of learning at work that help people understand the role of conflict.

Ironically, in the liberal democracy of the US, low-wage jobs are increasing and good jobs are vanishing, but most observers do not view this as class conflict. Most policy-makers look at the broad decline in wages and opportunity and propose to fix things with short-term job training, upgrading of job skills, and adult basic education. This mainly has the effect of increasing the number of unemployed workers available for low-wage jobs.

Finland is a country where a learning theory that draws on Marxist ideas of class conflict is mainstream. It is also a country where class conflict is muted by a very strong social welfare system, a large public sector, and a high rate of unionization. Today, almost seventy five percent of workers in Finland are in unions as compared to eleven percent in the United States. In Finland, *Activity theory* is used almost like a strategic planning tool in a business setting. In the US, where class conflict is masked but not muted, we can use it to help us see who is on our side and who is against us.

What is *Activity theory?*

Activity Theory proposes "an activity" as a unit of analysis. A unit of analysis means the minimum set of components that have to be taken into consideration in order to understand what's happening. It is like the molecule of a chemical compound, or the germ cell of a living organism. Andy Blunden, an educational researcher in Australia, proposes the term "project" instead of "activity," because it has many of the same meanings intended by "activity" and is more like ordinary speech. This also helps get away from possible confusions with behaviorism, since "activity" sounds a lot like "behavior." After all, you can observe someone's behavior and also someone's activity, so they can get confused. However, I will use the term *Activity Theory* because the best way to look it up on the internet is to use the term it is best known by.

An activity can be anything from designing a city to cooking a meal. The key to deciding what counts as an activity is identifying its purpose. If something contributes to the overall purpose of what is being done, it is part of that activity. If it does not, it is outside that activity system. In fact, it may be part of a different activity system, one that may either help ours or struggle with it.

Activity systems can share a purpose or be in conflict with each other. An example of two activity systems supporting each other would be when a church congregation offers sanctuary for a group of migrant workers. An example of two activity systems in conflict would be when workers, trying to raise their wages, get into a struggle with employers. For better or worse, these relationships are inevitably emotional. Emotions include anxiety, fear, anger, worry, gratitude, joy – the whole range of feelings that people have about their access to a job that provides them with a living. The knowledge that is created in this context of conflict is, therefore, charged with emotion that comes flooding back when the experience is remembered.

Other learning theories also have units of analysis, such as the learning cycle itself, or the community of practice, but those theories do not focus so sharply on defining the units of analysis. In *Activity Theory*, the unit of analysis is very specific and its edges, defined by purpose, are very clear. The whole activity is bounded by its purpose. You could think of the purpose as a river; everything that floats along that river is part of the activity. If we think about the migrant workers who have crossed the border to make a living in the fields, and the church congregation that is committed to helping desperate people make a decent living, their shared purpose is the river that they both float on.

The generic activity system is modeled by Engeström as a triangle. This model is familiar to everyone who draws on this theory. Like Kolb's learning cycle, it is easy to find on the web. It was first mapped out in Engeström's dissertation, *Learning by Expanding,* in 1987.

People tend to read this model in various ways. Here is how I read it (See Diagram 3, p 66). I begin with the line along the base, which is the community. Out of this community, through the process of division of labor (this is the lower right corner of the triangle), a set of people emerge who become the subjects of the activity. The word "subjects" here means the actors, the people who are doing the activity. The other meaning of the word "subject," as in a subject or topic, doesn't apply here. These subjects collectively have a purpose, a goal, which is represented by the line across the middle of the triangle from left to right. This goal (whether it is the immediate short-term object of the activity or the longer term or purpose) defines the whole activity system.

In order to accomplish this goal, the subjects use tools. The tools include all kinds of resources and can be anything, from hammers and nails to computers and technologies, including communications systems like telephones and languages. The tools "mediate" their activity. The subjects also have to carry out their activity within a context, which includes the history, customs, laws, and regulations that surround it. As time passes, these things may change and make new history.

As the subjects work toward the purpose of the activity system, things shift. A court case may change who can do what to whom. Leaders may get fired. A city politician may decide to speak up for the workers. Underlying disagreements and open conflicts occur. Alliances form and sometimes there is a lucky break. For example, when a historical tradition is revisited and reinterpreted, or when an important tool (like email or a website) is added, or when new people join the group of "subjects," the group can modify their approach to achieving the goal.

Diagram 3: Activity theory model (after Engestrom).

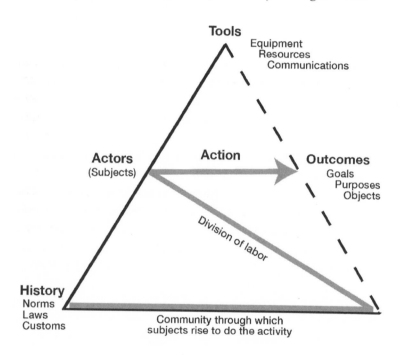

Engeström's arrangement of the components of this unit of analysis gives us a way to hold steady, study and explain the complex interactions of these components as the activity system (represented by the model) develops over time and responds to forces acting upon it. For people who have done power analysis exercises, the *Activity Theory* model, with its different components, will feel familiar.

Activity theory and hotel housekeepers

Suppose union leaders and staff have found out their members, workers who clean rooms and make beds in a certain hotel, are not taking breaks, even though by law they are entitled to a paid break every few hours. This is a significant injustice. This work schedule and room quota is resulting in repetitive stress injuries to workers' arms and backs. The union wants them to take breaks. The union also wants them to get paid retroactively for past work done during their breaks. The workers, mostly immigrant non-English speaking women, are unaware that they are entitled to breaks. Together, the union and the members try to figure out what has to happen in order for the workers to be able to take breaks and get their correct pay. These women come to the hotel and work, after all, to earn a living, not because they like pretty hotel rooms. Everything they decide to do to accomplish this goal is part of the activity system of what the housekeepers are doing in the hotels: trying to earn a living.

A lot of learning has to take place in order for this campaign to succeed. The workers have to learn that they are allowed to take breaks and should have been getting paid for breaks. They have to learn that breaks are required under U. S. law. They have to learn to connect working without breaks to their back and shoulder injuries. Then they have to learn how to openly support each other in taking breaks even when their supervisor berates and threatens them to keep them working.

The activity system of the housekeepers trying to avoid ergonomic injury by taking breaks comes into conflict with another activity system; in this case, the activity system of the management of the hotel. This is because the purpose of the management of the hotel is not the same as the purpose of the hotel housekeepers.

The purpose of the management is to run a successful business, which is defined as a profitable business. Letting workers take breaks will reduce the number of rooms they can clean. Paying them for those breaks will cost a lot of money.

Superficially, at any given moment, these two activity systems may be indistinguishable. When a housekeeper picks up wet towels and throws them in her laundry bag, she is both making the hotel successful and earning a living. But although these two activity systems may coincide in appearance, at the bottom, fundamentally, they diverge. The housekeeper needs her job to pay rent, buy groceries, and support her family. If she gets injured, she won't be able to keep working and earn a living, even a poor one. She has to think about these things first. They are more important to her than the profitability of the hotel.

It becomes clear that she has to survive the demands of her employer's activity system in order to accomplish the purposes of her own activity system.

One way to think of this is to remember that in order to succeed in one activity system (making a living), the housekeepers have to limit the number of ergonomic injuries they are suffering, because at a certain point it is just not possible to make any more beds, change any more pillowcases, push any more carts. This means that they have to push back in some way against the second activity system, the employer's desire to run a profitable hotel.

For months, or even years, the conflict between workers who are trying to make a living and employees or businesses that are trying to make a profit may be latent, but it always underlies worker-manager relationship. Activity theory defines their activity by its purpose, helps bring that conflict to the surface, and keeps it in the picture. In the case of the housekeepers, the conflict was suppressed because the housekeepers, before the union started to work on the problem, had no way to push back against their excessive workloads.

Like communities of practice, *Activity Theory* proposes that learning – or, more broadly speaking, social change, which depends on learning – takes place not in the individual mind or even in the transmission of information from one mind to another, but in a social interaction among people. It also takes as a given that none of these elements are stable. The people change, what they do changes, their tools and equipment change, and as time passes the rules they operate under change. The subjects in the group make their own history, building on what has gone before.

Of course, these changes mean that the balance of the system shifts, cracks appear, and new relationships throw old agreements into knots. Sometimes opportunities arise. A new tool – a newsletter, a database, an office – changes who knows what and who has access to what. New activists emerge from the "community" and challenge the balance of power in the leadership. A new law is passed or an old law is disputed and erased, changing the history of the context. A new group of workers are hired who don't speak English and someone has to be found to talk with them. This is the normal forward movement over time of any activity system. By looking back on and interpreting these changes, people learn.

Here is a simplified account of a workplace situation to show how *Activity Theory* can be used to figure out what is going on and what might be done about a specific problem.

As the economy worsened during 2005-6, an office of state welfare caseworkers came under pressure to serve more clients. In the past, names were called off a waiting list, and the client whose name was called would walk from the waiting room to the cubicle of their caseworker. The time spent calling off the waiting list consumed up to five minutes per individual. The manager decided that, to save time, caseworkers would walk out from their cubicles to the waiting room and interview clients in their chairs in the waiting room. Caseworkers resisted, saying they needed to work at their desks where their papers were filed, that the "lost" five minutes were necessary for paperwork, and that clients interviewed in the waiting room would lose all privacy.

Here again are two activity systems in conflict, one focusing on increasing production (the manager's perspective) and the other focusing on preserving the conditions under which caseworkers could carry out their work in an effective and ethical manner. Neither side was clearly in full opposition to the other. After all, both caseworkers and management wanted to serve as many clients as possible. Management saw this as a production issue; the caseworkers, including their union leaders, saw it as a matter of professional standards.

There was a standoff. Neither side would budge. However, management feared trying to impose discipline and force the caseworkers to comply.

The caseworkers then printed T-shirts with the word "respect" in big letters, both back and front, and wore them to work. One of the effects of this was to engage the clients on the side of the caseworkers and make them aware of the problem. At this, management backed off.

In the language of *Activity Theory*, the T-shirts would be a "tool." The caseworkers took control of the narrative by publicly reframing the situation as an issue of professional standards, which trumped, for the moment, the management focus on production. The T-shirt "tool" was a way to make the issue visible to the public in a way that resembled silent picketing while at work. The word "respect" was so non-controversial that the managers did not risk the embarrassment of forbidding it.

Learning was taking place throughout the confrontation. It happened during the initial reaction to management's proposal (the "event" from *Kolb's Learning Cycle*), during the planning phase (where they built *Work Process Knowledge*), during the day when people wore their T-shirts (and acted as a *Community of Practice*, drawing in both clients and new hires who didn't know much about the union) and later, when looking back on their success. It also happened when they chose to add the T-shirt to their tools, which drew the *activity system* of the clients (trying to get service) into alignment with the activity system of the caseworkers.

Making the learning visible

With these four theories in mind, we can start to make visible the knowledge that people create in the process of doing their work. We can begin to account for the shock experienced by the three teachers described in Chapter 2 when they heard the stationary engineers assert that no one would ever quibble if they warned that something was going wrong. We can begin to envision what is going on when someone who has been laid off after working for thirty years suddenly starts to talk passionately about his job. We can understand why someone who has worked at the back end of a restaurant kitchen, washing the pots, might claim that he has "learned how to run a restaurant – backwards!" We can begin to appreciate the resistance workers are likely to demonstrate when asked to do something that violates this knowledge or disrespects it. We can also conceive of how sharing this knowledge can build connections among workers from various workplaces in order to improve their work and their lives.

This knowledge is not always a blessing. Sometimes it is a burden. I have a friend who was a shop chair—an elected

Table 1. Comparison of questions prompted by theories.

Kolb's Learning Cycle	Communities of Practice
What happened?	What is the practice?
How do we explain what happened?	Who is in the community of practice and who is outside it? What are its edges?
What does this (the thing that happened) mean to us?	Are newcomers welcome? Are they given real work to do? Does everyone know about the path from beginner to expert, outsider to insider? Is the path public and transparent or private and hidden? Are we developing leaders that can keep things going?
What should we do?	Are we going to make it?

Work Process Knowledge	Activity Theory
What is the problem?	What is the purpose of the activity system? Who is the community?
Who else is touched by this problem? Can we reach them and include them in a network? What does the problem look like to them?	What activity systems are aligned with this one? What activity systems are opposed to or in conflict with it? What is their purpose?
What is supposed to happen, what is actually happening, and what is the difference? What is the history of this problem – here and in other places? What tools and resources do we need? Should anyone else be involved in this?	What tools do we have? What tools can we create? How does history, ours and theirs, constrain or increase the possibilities we can choose from? Can we re-frame the situation in some way to our advantage?
Are we ready to test our solution?	Where should we expect to see stresses and conflicts as we make changes in order to move forward? Are we ready to deal with them?

workplace leadership position—in a factory for many years. This was a garment factory in rural Pennsylvania where about 160 workers sewed pants. When the factory closed, the only job she could find was non-union retail. As a shop chair, she was a good organizer. She could plan strategy. She knew a lot about labor law and employment regulations. In her new job, she could look at the whole store, its stock, its workforce, its schedule and its customers. She could see how things ought to be organized and where the problems were. She knew how she could fix things to make it easier and better for the workers. In addition, she knew how to make the whole place run better. She was also silently critical of both the store and the corporate management. This knowledge was part of her character.

Her new co-workers sensed this knowledge in her but she had to conceal it. She could not share it, for risk of being spotted by management as a troublemaker. Possessing this knowledge but being unable to share it made her lonely at work. She told me that at her new job, "Other workers can tell I know something and they come to me. They bring me problems. But I can't say anything. I have to keep my mouth shut."

She told me that this was the most painful part about working non-union, even more painful than making less than $10 per hour.

What questions do these theories help us ask?

Theories are blunt instruments. Sometimes, when you bring a theory to a real life situation and try to use it, the effect is to oversimplify what you are observing.

One way to try to preserve the complexity of real life situations is to ask some questions in a sequence prompted by each theory. Table 1 shows how I would go about doing that. I can imagine a group of people facing a problem who get together and use these questions as a discussion guide. (Please see Table 1 pp 72-73.)

CHAPTER 6:
TARZAN: A BAD THEORY

Once off the path, one's wanderings are endless.
— Chinese saying

Not all theories are any good.

Suppose you follow the steps of *Kolb's Learning Cycle* and some information is missing, your categories are wrong, you don't test your ideas enough, and you come up with an analysis that is wrong – what will happen? You've created a bad theory and now you want to act on it. Is anyone going to get hurt? Probably.

A bad theory will lead you and everyone around you into all kinds of trouble. Just for comparison, here is an example of a bad theory. This theory essentially says that if you are white and try hard you can learn, even if you are completely alone. What matters is willpower, attitude, and "good" genetics. It helps if you are English nobility. This is a good theory if you want to design a school system that sorts out a very few to succeed, and lets most people fail.

The book *Tarzan of the Apes*, by Edgar Rice Burroughs, was published first in 1912, just before World War I. It takes place in Africa. At that time all of Africa, except for Liberia and Ethiopia, was under European colonial rule. This book was enormously popular. It was reprinted hundreds of times and read by generations of young people. The original book was followed by dozens of sequels and re-created as cartoons, stage plays and films.

Narratives with this kind of staying power usually reflect some level of popular consensus about reality and how things work. At the very least, they cannot radically diverge from something that people at least hope is possible, no matter whether it seems astonishing or even miraculous. The psychologist Jerome Bruner, in *Actual Minds, Possible Worlds* (1986), writes:

> For stories define the range of canonical characters, the settings in which they operate, the actions that are permissible and comprehensible. And thereby they provide, so to speak, a map of possible roles and of possible worlds in which action, thought, and self-definition are permissible (or desirable) (1986, p. 66).

They provide, in other words, a kind of general theory of human nature. Bruner, incidentally, was among the psychologists instrumental in bringing Vygotsky's work to the United States in the 1960s.

So here is a general theory of learning that did not arouse skepticism at the time, that was accepted as "permissible and comprehensible" in a kind of archetypical way both when it was published and even after Africa emerged from under colonial rule. Something about the Tarzan story apparently still makes sense to people, given the persistence of the Tarzan story in movies being made in recent years. The Tarzan story is embodied in many aspects of current efforts at school reform as well.

What Tarzan says about how people learn

According to *Tarzan of the Apes,* learning is the result of willpower. If you try, you learn. If you don't learn, it's because you didn't try. However, you also have to be smart. Some people are born smart and some aren't. If you try and you don't learn, you're stupid and there's nothing you can do about it.

According to this theory, knowledge gets printed into the human brain through brute effort, as if the mind was a kind of photocopying machine floating in space.

Here is the story. You will find it only told once, in the first book.

Tarzan is the infant son of British aristocrats who have been deposited from their ship by mutineers somewhere on the coast of Africa. He is orphaned in infancy and adopted by the giant ape Kala. The only language he hears is ape-speech. Then at the age of ten, Tarzan discovers the cabin that his parents built before they died, breaks in, finds a cupboard full of books, in English, and teaches himself to read. How does he do that?

Many of the books are children's books and have pictures, which he at first tries to pick off the page.

> ...the odd little figures which appeared beneath and between the colored pictures – some strange kind of bug he thought they might be, for many of them had legs though nowhere could he find one with eyes and a mouth. It was his first introduction to the letters of the alphabet, and he was over ten years old.
>
> Of course he had never before seen print, or never had spoken with any living thing which had the remotest idea or that such a thing as a written language existed, nor ever had he seen anyone reading (p.43).

Months after his first encounter with books, Tarzan returns to the cabin and gets them out again. Burroughs tells us that they "seemed to exert a strange and powerful influence over him, so that he could scarce attend to aught else for the lure of the wondrous puzzle which their purpose presented to him" (48). Burroughs later attributes this to the fact that he is, genetically, an English gentleman. Tarzan squats over the book, examining the "bugs."

> And so he progressed very slowly, for it was a
> hard and laborious task which he had set himself
> without knowing it – a task which might seem to
> you or me impossible… (p.49).

Reading, is of course, the code of codes: every single level of its innumerable concentric shells of code has a key which must be given to the learner by someone who already has it. Examples of this include the fact that sentences go from left to right horizontally across a page, there are spaces between words, and many letters (not all, because English is not phonetic) are connected to sounds. You can't figure this out yourself because there's no way to test if you're right or wrong. Someone has to tell you. The only way to test if you are saying something meaningful is to see if anyone understands you. Because of this, educators speak of learning to read as being "contagious," in the sense that knowing how to do it is passed from one person to another.

In Tarzan's case, however, he is alone. No one can give him any keys to any codes. Instead, "learning" turns into "grasping" which turns into "knowing":

> He did not accomplish it in a day, or in a week or
> in a month or in a year, but slowly, very slowly,
> he learned after he had grasped the possibilities
> which lay in those little bugs, so that by the time
> he was fifteen he knew the various combinations
> of letters which stood for every pictured figure in
> the little primer and in one or two of the picture
> books (p. 49).

After seven years:

> By the time he was seventeen he had learned

80

to read the simple child's primer and had fully realized the true and wonderful purpose of the little bugs. No longer did he feel shame for his hairless body or his human features, for now his reason told him that he was a different race from his wild and hairy companions. He was an M-A-N, they were A-P-E-S, and the little apes which scurried through the forest top were M-O-N-K-E-Y-S. ...And so he learned to read. From then on his progress was rapid. With the help of the great dictionary and the active intelligence of a healthy mind endowed by inheritance with more than ordinary reasoning power he shrewdly guessed at much which he could not really understand, and more often than not his guesses were close to the mark of truth (p. 50).

He has gone from "trying" to "grasping" to "knowing" to "fully realizing the true and wonderful purpose" and "guessing the truth" – all by hard work. By eighteen he has effectively educated himself:

At eighteen he read fluently and understood nearly all he read in the many and varied volumes on the shelves...Thus at eighteen we find him, an English lordling, who could speak no English, and yet who could read and write his native language. Never had he seen a human other than himself, for the little area traversed by his tribe was watered by no greater river to bring down the savage natives from the interior (p. 62).

Embedded in the Tarzan story is a theory of how people learn that is rarely expressed in words but often shows up being applied in real life. This theory says, simply, that learning is an individual activity. You break the code for yourself. If you try hard enough, and keep at it, learning will happen. Self-discipline is the key. Nothing else is required – no teacher, no coach, no one to discuss things with. If you fail, it is because you didn't try hard enough and it is your fault. It helps, of course, if you have a certain genetic assets – specifically, if you are a member of the English aristocracy. For some reason, having the DNA of an English lord will help you learn to read if you are abandoned in infancy in a jungle.

What is the Tarzan theory?

The theory behind the practice of teaching by information transfer is this: when a person is presented with information, by exposure to it, the information is learned, or "internalized," as the term goes. Failing to learn, failing a test, is the result of not trying hard enough. "Trying hard" becomes a moral strategy. When someone doesn't learn what they are supposed to learn, it's got nothing to do with the world they live in; it's all about lack of willpower and bad attitude.

The difference between theories that are neighbors and cousins of the *Tarzan Theory* and the four theories in Chapter 5 is that the four theories I like say that learning happens through social interaction, through discussion, trial and error, the power of community, the creation or destruction of tools, conflict and new history, and that power matters. None of the theories I have presented have anything to do with trying hard or being intellectually gifted.

The *Tarzan Theory* also flows naturally into extreme racist presumptions. You will have to read the book itself to see what I mean. You will be appalled.

At its best, the Tarzan approach to learning just sorts people. Sorting goes on in schools today as a product of standardized testing. Students, teachers and schools are separated into categories according to test scores. At work, for the purposes of teaching people how to defend themselves, their jobs and their colleagues, sorting is deadly. Anything that separates or isolates people who share a need to earn a living is a mistake.

Instead, what is wanted is a way to break the code and spread the news as if it were a contagious disease. A sense of common purpose should be expanded to encompass something that can become a community. Problems, if they are not insurmountable, feed the strength of the community if they are used to contribute to collective sense-making and commitment. Paths to leadership, both temporary and flexible or long-term and stable, must be transparently visible to participants. Points of conflict, consequences that flow from changes in tools, strategies, equipment and norms have to be out in the open for people to talk about.

For those readers who are familiar with Freire's work, the Tarzan approach will sound a lot like the "banking" model of learning, in which a student is treated like a bank into which the teacher "deposits" information the way you deposit money into a bank. The student is supposed to withdraw the information later, on a test, the way you withdraw your money from a bank. Of course, this does not work.

Ironically, since we are talking about Tarzan, there is something else to say about the difference between humans and apes. The reason humans have been able to develop mentally beyond our primate cousins is because we learn collaboratively. "Chimps seem to lack the impulse toward collective problem-solving that is so central to human society," reports Elizabeth Kolbert in *The Sixth Extinction* (p. 249). Intelligence is inherited only in the sense that humans have a genetic disposition to communicate and act socially. Kolbert refers to Michael Tomasello, who heads the Department of Development and Comparative Psychology at the Institution for Evolutionary Anthropology in Leipzig.

Tomasello makes the point that chimps do a lot of incredibly smart things, but the main difference between chimps and human beings is that people "put their heads together." He notes that if you put a heavy log in a chimp cage, you will never see two chimps pick it up and carry it together.

In other words, Tarzan never learned to read. It didn't happen. He grew old and died in his nest in the tree.

The rest of the chapters in this book are about real-life situations. In these chapters people deal with problems collaboratively, take their time, strategize and learn from what they've done.

CHAPTER 7:
EFFINGHAM: BOMB, UNION, STRIKE, LOCKOUT, CONTRACT

"I still glance out my kitchen window to see the picket shed that still reads NEVER GIVE UP! It has been and still is an inspiration to me and my whole family." — Gail Warner

In this chapter we will talk about people who had to start their union from scratch. I will use this to illustrate *Kolb's learning cycle*, but this is a true story that spills over any theory into the deep grass of real life. There is a clear "event" or experience. Then there is a period of sorting things out. This is followed by the development of an analysis and a strategy. The strategy gets put into practice. Then it goes around again – event, sorting things out, figuring out what's going on, figuring out what to do, and another event. Actually, it's not just a cycle, it's a spiral. It takes years – it's a struggle – but eventually there is a sort of conclusion and victory, a successful test of the strategy. This spiral stretched out across a calendar cycle of years.

There are also clear examples of how a *community of practice* works in this story, as well as moments when *Activity theory* is helpful for noting how changes in tools and laws and regulations change the balance of power. Ultimately, the negotiation of a contract is what seals the achievements of the struggle by changing the rules of the social relationships of this workplace.

Each change in the balance of power is an event, triggering discussions and ideas about how to respond or what to do next. You can also see how the *Work Process Knowledge* of the workers builds into collective competence, complete with risks of betrayal.

Heartland Human Services is in Effingham, Illinois, two hundred miles south of Chicago. Effingham lies at the crossroads of two Interstate highways, in the middle of fabulously rich agricultural land. It is famous for a giant white cross, 198 feet high, just south of town that is visible for miles around and on YouTube. Heartland is a not-for-profit, privately owned, full-service four-county mental health agency, the only agency of its kind in the area. It serves the working class of Effingham, or, as Lucille Musser, one of the original organizers who later became president of the union, put it, "The poor and the near-poor." Heartland has a reputation of serving the ne'er-do-wells, the people on public aid, the jail docket and the drinkers. It has a group home for boys, a residential home for men and women who are mentally ill, services for people who are developmentally disabled, and counseling for county probation, state parole and federal probation systems. It provides AIDS training, substance abuse prevention, child abuse prevention, classes in anger management, teen pregnancy prevention and services for children of divorcing parents.

In 2006, when this story begins, at Effingham there was no union, no contract, no structure of representation, no history of consult and confer, and no written policy that couldn't be changed unilaterally by management when it wanted to. Instead, there was rumor, custom, and habit, guessing about what the boss wanted, and "our way of doing things." The jobs overall were decent jobs, however. People stayed at this place for a lifetime. There aren't many jobs in Central Illinois, so one reason they stayed was because there weren't many other places to go.

The people at Heartland Health Services made a transition from a situation where nothing could be taken for granted to one where there was a framework in place, in this case a union contract, all in five years. The transition was a rough ride and the outcome was never assured. When it began, people on both labor and management sides were taking a step off a cliff. Furthermore, figuring out what winning would really mean was not easy or obvious. The whole fight was an intense learning experience, often painful, for everyone involved.

Three important terms: Public sector, private sector, and service sector

The National Labor Relations Act of 1935, which came into being to provide a legal framework for agreements between employers and workers, only covered workplaces in the private sector, and not even all of those. For example, agricultural workers and domestic workers were excluded. Most public sector workplaces were not covered by labor law until the 1960s or later, and this coverage took place state-by-state, not in every state at once.

"Public sector" means places where tax revenues support the work that is carried out, like city, state and county offices, public schools or hospitals, transportation authorities, police and fire departments or public colleges and universities. It does not mean companies that have "gone public" in the sense of offering to sell shares in the stock market. It also does not mean services that are open to the public, like roads or parks. This is important background to this chapter because Heartland provides a service that is historically public (tax-funded) but in this case is owned as a private business. Thus we are going to talk about work that historically belonged to the public sector and that became part of the private sector. In other words, it was "privatized" by being contracted out to a private employer. This was part of a long-term shift of public assets and services into the private sector, supposedly to gain efficiency, but also to make them profitable for someone. This is relevant to the story because the union that eventually succeeded in getting a contract at Heartland was

AFSCME, the American Federation of State, County and Municipal Employees, which historically represents public sector workers. AFSCME has a practice of "following the work" and organizing workers whose jobs have become privatized.

The term "service sector" is also important. "Service" is usually contrasted with "industrial" sector, or manufacturing. "Service" jobs are jobs where people take care of, wait on, or help other people rather than building houses or making cars. They may be jobs in hotels and restaurants, retail, beauty salons or prisons, among others, and many are jobs in health and human services, like the jobs at Heartland.

Although lawyers and doctors are also "service workers," service jobs are usually low-wage. Back in the 1980s, when people began to become aware of the impact of globalization, we recognized that as we lost our manufacturing and industrial base, we risked becoming an economy based on service jobs. However, there was optimism that we might become a "knowledge" or "information" economy, drawing on our solid education system and tradition of innovation and entrepreneurship (see Robert Reich, *The Work of Nations: Preparing ourselves for 21st Century Capitalism*, Knopf 1992). Then, as our economy became more and more integrated into the global flow of finance, high-skill workers with good educations emerged in countries all over the world and "knowledge" jobs – it was clear that "knowledge" meant "tech" – flowed to meet them. The majority of the jobs that stayed in the US were the service jobs. These jobs stay here because they serve people who are here.

The Town Fathers of Effingham

The area around Effingham is conservative, Catholic, Lutheran, and Baptist. It is also like many such towns in that it was until recently a "sundown" town, where black people were not welcome after sundown. Today, Effingham is still mostly white. It is not a poor town: there is quite a bit of money there, but it is old money and it's in the hands of people referred to by the workers as "the town fathers." These people do not rely on public services: they can afford to go elsewhere for vacations, education and healthcare.

A lot of the businesses are passed down through families and carry family names, mostly German, not chain store names. In fact, the small suburb to the east of Effingham is named Teutopolis, settled by German Catholics in the 1840's. Being German still corresponds with relative wealth: median household income is $47,450 per year in Teutopolis compared to Effingham's $34,761 per year.

Effingham is isolated both by geography and by intention. It is not a "union-based community." The public schools, the railroad and the Post Office are the only union jobs in town. "Bringing a union in is like breaking a holy law," says one of the women who worked at the health center. "The city fathers have got the unions out and kept them out." Other towns in the rural Midwest have reported the same experience.

Previously unionized workplaces have left Effingham – Worldcolor Press, Crossroads Press, and Fedder's Air Conditioning are gone. Kingery Printing went bankrupt. If someone has enough money to run a business here, he can also afford to say that if a union comes in, he'll shut the doors.

A worker who eventually went on strike during this struggle at Heartland Human Services said, "He's made his money. He can close his place of business and go home and live off the interest of his investments." The same person confirmed that Toyota was going to locate there but, "the city fathers kept it out because, they knew it would raise salaries." Another story told how there was a company that made airplane brakes that was going to train their own people and would pay $20 an hour. Even though it wasn't union, the city fathers kept it out. They didn't want a high-wage company coming into town and drawing workers away from low-wage jobs. This is a distorted but not unusual role for a small-city economic development planning board. In fact, in January 2014, Republicans in the Tennessee state legislature threatened to cut tax incentives and subsidies to the Volkswagen plant in Chattanooga if workers there voted to bring in the United Auto Workers (UAW).

Labor has a long and bitter history in Effingham. Like many towns in Central Illinois, it was once a mining town. Back in the 1930s during the mining wars, when the Progressive Miners broke away from the United Mine Workers, the railroad that still passes through town was blown up. Some say the dynamite was planted by Peabody, the company that owned the mine and the same company as the one in the John Prine song "Down by the Green River." Peabody is still the main owner and operator of coal mines in Illinois, although they are now all non-union. They were recently in the news for spinning off their retiree obligations into a small sub-company, which then declared bankruptcy.

While the division of the town into two classes, "the city fathers" and the working class, was known to the workers before they began their fight, it was perceived as background history and culture. Before the strike, they did not understand how far this division would reach into their workplace. Nor did they anticipate the lengths to which the city fathers would go to keep them from winning.

How Heartland Human Services is funded

During the period in the 1970s, when public health services were spun off into community-based operations, Heartland was set up as a private non-profit. Therefore, at the time of this story it fell under private sector labor law, the National Labor Relations Act of 1935. Although it is privately owned, it is funded entirely by fees, grants and state and local public money from the Department of Human Services, Social Security, Medicaid and Medicare. Heartland bills its clients on a sliding fee scale, and it has a Community Development Program to provide free services to the indigent. The one other social service agency in town that has a program for people with developmental disabilities can only handle a few clients.

At the time that the events in this story took place, Heartland was overseen by a Board of Directors consisting of seven people, four men and three women. They were an Assistant Superintendent of Schools, President of a Baptist Church, a minister, a retired teacher and a nurse who manages a hospital. The "town fathers" hired the Director, who then selected the board.

The boss is the best organizer

In October, 2005, an event took place that Heartland workers call "the bomb."

The Director of Heartland, a woman who had herself worked for Heartland for over twenty years, called a meeting of everyone who worked there. At that time, it employed about 160 people. According to several Heartland workers, they all went down to the basement meeting room, where chairs were set up. The Director announced that she would take no questions. She passed out a sheet of paper. Saying they were in a financial crisis, she told the employees what she was going to do in order to avoid this crisis. Then she "dropped this bomb," as one worker put it, walked out of the room and went to Europe on vacation. She had previously arranged to have police outside the building, as if she was afraid that there would be a violent reaction from the employees about the announcement.

The workers first had to figure out how what was contained in the "bomb" was going to affect them. It meant drastic changes in their work, including wage cuts, loss of benefits, work hour increases, and reductions in holidays. The whole agency would shift from funding entire programs to fee-for-service billing. The work week increased from 35 hours to 40 hours. All the benefits for part-time workers were taken away. Before the Director's announcement, people had vacation, holidays, sick days and personal days. One woman who had worked there 35 years had accumulated 20 vacation days, 12 holidays, 12 sick days and 3 personal days. After the Director was done with this announcement, that same woman had 20 "personal time off" days per year – period.

Two particularly problematic changes were the establishment of productivity standards and a new on-call system. A productivity standard establishes a goal for the amount of work done. Case managers, counselors and therapists were all going to have to meet productivity standards, as would anyone else who did billable work. The issue usually arises over what the unit of measurement of the work should be. Should the work of a therapist, for example, be measured by hours spent, by phone calls answered, patients met, patients referred, or patients cured? This all flowed from the change from entire program funding to fee for service/billable hours funding.

According to union organizer Lucille Musser, if you met your productivity goal, you would get a bonus. You had to be seeing people face to face or doing case management on the phone in order for an interaction to be billable, and 65% of your time had to be billable. Your paperwork had to be finished within 24 hours. You had to make two marketing calls on your own time. If a patient didn't show up or missed an appointment, you didn't get credit, even if you were in your office, waiting for the patient. You could get fired if you didn't "do productivity." The productivity standards created paranoia and encouraged cheating. Some workers who were doing "overhead" rather than "billable" work tried to help people who were "on productivity" work. This was an attempt to work together to benefit each other. But that was not a long-term solution.

The new on-call arrangement was especially burdensome. An on-call rotation was established. You would be on call at night. You had to use your own cell phone, assuming you had one. For being on call, you would get $1.75 per hour. If you got called out, you got time and a half based on your pay rate. You would not have a choice about being on call. If you were called out at night and were out all night, you still had to work the next day, or else take one of your personal time off days. If you were too tired to work it would be an "unexcused absence." One worker who had been there 15 years was soon fired for refusing to take the on-call schedule. He had a doctor's note saying that he had to get a good night's sleep. The Director fired him, saying, "You can't do the job."

There were a lot of other new rules as well. Some of them seemed capricious, such as requiring employees to walk residents from their rooms to group meetings, but then also accompany them to the bathroom, which meant leaving the group without a staff person.

The workers were angry, frustrated and insulted. They were afraid to go over the Director's head to the Board. They knew they'd get fired if they sent a message and signed their own names.

Everyone has heard that the cost of healthcare has been rising and that state and federal funding for all kinds of programs has been cut and may disappear completely in the next few years. Therefore agencies like Heartland, in order to keep going at all, have to find ways to cut costs. Strategies for cutting costs are well-known. However, the Director of Heartland appears to have tried to implement them all at the same time, unilaterally.

The first reaction of many of the workers was, *"Can she do that?"* The answer is, of course, yes. But this first phase was one of general confusion, as workers tried to figure out what had happened and how it was going to affect everyone.

Figuring out what happened, starting to organize

As soon as the "bomb" dropped, people started talking with each other, with their families, at their churches and with friends. According to Lucille Musser, four of the Heartland workers started thinking about organizing a union right away. They were two men and two women. One, Anna Beck, had worked in a union workplace before. Another, Gail Warner, had a brother who was a union electrician. The other two knew people who worked in union workplaces. This meant that they had a general idea that being in a union would give them some protection against capricious changes in their working conditions. These four were the most experienced in terms of thinking about unions out of the whole 160-person workforce. This gave them a standpoint from which to start to figure out what had just been done to them. Like most Americans, the other workers had never really understood what a union was. Many simply accepted without question the opinion of the town fathers that unions were mob-driven, third-party nuisances that would attract lawyers and cause businesses to leave town.

At the beginning, the attempts to make collective sense of a confusing and frightening situation were on an each-one-teach-one basis. It was a matter of sorting things out, on the one hand, and combatting misinformation on the other. The content of what was being taught and learned changed with every new problem that cropped up. How should workers respond to the part-time workers who had suddenly lost their benefits? How should they deal with co-workers who were on this new productivity standard and would lose money if a client failed to show up? When the time came, who should make the phone call to a national union asking for help, and what should they tell them? Which national union should they call? Who should come to the first meeting, and where should it be held, and who should know about it? What should they expect? How should they treat their clients, many of whom relied desperately on getting their medication, therapy, or other kinds of treatment, whom they were likely to encounter in a grocery store or at church or on the street? What would they say when the client asked, "What is going on at Heartland?" How would they explain it?

Every one of these decisions was part of making sense out of their *experience* of "the bomb" that had blasted away their confidence that they had decent jobs in a decent workplace. This was the first step around the learning cycle.

The team of four made telephone calls, held discussions and meetings over coffee, and amazingly enough, by December, 2005, the organizers knew that although people were scared, 98% of them were on board. While they did not know much about unions, they did know that what the Director had imposed on them was intolerable. The team decided it was time to take the next step, which was to get in touch with an "official" union. They chose AFSCME, the American Federation of State, County and Municipal Employees. AFSCME responded. This does not always happen. Only too often, workers will be looking for a union to represent them and they pick a union out of the phone book and the union says no, thanks. Sometimes this is because the union itself is already strapped for money or overextended. However, AFSCME's big strength is in the public sector. As public work is increasingly privatized out, it has become critical for the union to follow the work no matter where it goes. AFSCME sent one full-time and several part-time staff down to Effingham, opened an office in the center of town, and got to work.

If the first step around the cycle was figuring out what

had happened and explaining it to the rest of the workforce, and the second step was deciding that they were ready to call in a national union, we could say that the third step, the "experiment" or "applied" phase of the learning cycle was the vote. Had the organizers assessed the workforce correctly? Would the 98% who seemed to be on board vote for the union? The election was held in February 2006. Anger was more powerful than fear. In choosing between voting for "no union" or representation by AFSCME, the workers at Heartland voted for representation.

Curiously, the Director never really fought the organizing campaign. According to Heartland workers, they learned later that she didn't think it would happen. There were two main programs at Heartland, residential and outpatient, and the Director never anticipated that the employees in one program would talk with employees in the other. But they did. They conspired.

Bargaining Begins

Now a new cycle of learning started. Once a workforce has had an election and brings in a union, they still don't have a contract. To get a contract, you have to bargain with the employer. Now that they had learned how to organize, they had to learn how to *bargain*.

At this point, the workers had learned about their labor rights in a climate of fighting, fear and worry. Effingham was a city where "You're breaking a holy law" when you bring in a union. It was a city where the only workers with union representation were teachers, postal workers, and railroad workers, and where unionized workplaces had been run out of town. But like any battle, people who are in it together become close friends. This means that the *collective competence* that is being created when these people call each other up, talk in the parking lot, run into each other at church or talk over family dinners, is very emotionally charged.

It's impossible, for example, for someone to ask, "How are things going at work?" without the other person thinking about the part-time employee who has suddenly lost her health insurance, or the residents who are affected by the preoccupation of the workers with their new working conditions. This means that the workers are not only learning a great deal about the legal and historic context of employment relations in the US, including things like how to run a union election under the National Labor Relations Board and who this strangely-named national union called AFSCME actually is. They are gaining knowledge by taking a crash course that is emotionally charged, because people are having to take sides, look at the town fathers through different eyes, make friends and trust people who were just co-workers only a few months ago, and speak up in ways that they have not ever done before.

There will be people who are scared to death, sure that they will be fired or harassed. There will be people whose paychecks support a whole family or extended family, a condition that was becoming increasingly common in central Illinois at that time. There will be people who are risking not only their own income, but money that others depend on. The knowledge that they acquire in the process of organizing is infused with this emotion. The sum total of this is what is meant by "class consciousness."

But they now have to move forward, which means that they have to negotiate a contract. A contract is an agreement between workers as a collectivity and their employer. The contract will govern the new social relationships of their workplace, which in the past were ungoverned and at the will or whim of their employer, as they found out when she dropped "the bomb." The union staffers assigned to Effingham, knowledgeable about how this was supposed to happen, provided the workers with a map and told them what to expect.

Then they tried to bargain, and the Director refused to meet with them. She either failed to show up for meetings, postponed meetings, or came to the table unprepared, saying that she had not read their materials. The negotiating committee kept coming back and coming back. Over and over, the AFSCME staffers talked the members through the stalemate. A core article in the National Labor Relations Act (and in all the public sector bargaining laws that are based on it) says that parties have to "bargain in good faith." "Bargaining" means moving past your starting position, making concessions, coming up with new ideas, compromising, finding common ground and being creative. Good bargainers do all this. The "in good faith" part means showing up on time, doing your homework, sincerely committing to the process, making yourself available, sharing information. "Bad faith bargaining" – in which a party does not do these things – is a violation of the NLRA. Once you are in the universe of having a union and are under the purview of a Labor Board, violating that law creates a flow of problems.

The bargaining at Heartland proceeded in ways that looked to the union like bad faith bargaining. The Director and the management team failed to do all those things listed above. Then the union invited a mediator to come in. A mediator is someone with advanced training in the bargaining process who is officially neutral. They come from the Federal Mediation and Conciliation Service (FMCS). The FMCS was established as part of the 1948 legislation known as Taft-Hartley for the purpose of creating more paths to negotiated agreements. Their service is federally funded and free to users. The idea is that the money saved overall by expediting an agreement is worth the cost of providing a mediator, given that the economy depends on people having jobs and going to work. The mediator made a contract proposal which was acceptable to the Heartland workers but which the Heartland management rejected.

Because of Heartland's evident failure to bargain in good faith, the union filed charges of unfair labor practices at the National Labor Relations Board. However, the charges were rejected by the regional Board in St. Louis. When I asked why these charges were rejected, the union was unwilling to speculate why, except that under President George Bush, appointments to the NLRB had become extremely politicized and openly anti-union. So the attempts to bargain continued, with no muscle being applied from the NRLB to move them faster toward a contract.

Finally, in July, 2007, over a year after they organized, the workers gave the Director thirty days to come to the table, warning her that if she didn't come, they would go on strike.

She didn't show up.

They went on strike.

We can think of this as the third time around the *Learning Cycle*.

Strike

This is a workforce of people who are mostly female and fundamentally caregivers, not fighters. In the span of less than two years, however, driven by the shock of "the bomb" and the astonishing contempt shown toward them by the Director and the Board, they were picketing.

Throughout this whole process, most workers stayed involved. No more than five people crossed the line and went back to work. Some had to get other jobs and participated in the strike activity only sparingly. Others made it the central activity of their lives. They held rallies, spoke with the local media, got on the radio, passed out flyers, went door-knocking. Teachers from the teachers' union (the Illinois Education Association) walked their picket line, let them use the bathroom in their union office and gave them money. Some of the workers practiced public speaking and learned to make presentations. They went to other unions, to conferences and union conventions in other cities and spoke from the podium to audiences of thousands. They talked on the radio and on TV. They wrote letters to the editor and did interviews.

As it got colder, workers set up a strike hut in front of Heartland Human Services and staffed it. The few employees who crossed the line, plus some who were hired after the strike started, had to drive past them. The strikers went out to the street and tried to talk to them as they drove past. When the snow fell, the strikers sat in the strike hut and warmed themselves at a propane burner. This was the point at which I met them.

I had come down to Effingham to talk with a railroad worker about a labor education class for railroad safety representatives. The railroad worker took me on a walk along the Illinois Central tracks. He showed me what good and bad ballast looked like, and explained how a signal post two hundred miles away, in Indiana, could be a fatal hazard to someone riding a train through Effingham. Then I asked him if he knew about the Heartland workers. He said he did, and added that he had spoken brusquely on their behalf to one of the members of the Board of Directors, the Baptist minister, while playing golf with him only a few days before. He told me where their strike hut was.

There they were, in deep snow, huddled in a white tent over a propane gas heater. Three women were there. Several more were walking up and down outside the tent picketing. Our conversation was quick, since they had no idea who I was or why I was dropping in on them, except that I was a labor educator from the university. I asked if they'd come to a women's conference I was organizing later the next spring, in May 2008, and they signed on immediately. Their attitude suggested that they were ready for anything. Luckily, the conference, the Regina Polk Conference, was fully funded by money raised in honor of a young organizer with the Teamsters who was killed while working, so there was scholarship money that would support their attendance. My plan was to build a role-playing exercise for the conference around what was going on at Heartland. They did in fact come to the conference and presented their experience to date.

By midsummer 2008, one year after the strike began, with no movement at all taking place at the bargaining table, the workers faced another choice. According to law, if a union and an employer cannot come to agreement and bargain a contract successfully within one year of the union getting organized, the employer can call for another vote by employees on whether or not they want union representation. This is called a decertification vote. The people who would be able to vote would be the workers who were currently employed at Heartland – that is, the five who had crossed the picket line plus those who had been hired after the strike began. It was highly likely they would decertify the union.

The Heartland strikers, in other words, risked finding that their union was gone. Therefore, after a year of being on strike, they decided to go back in and offer to return to work, unconditionally. The meeting in which they agreed to do this was intense and emotional. They talked about how they would act and what they would say to the people who had crossed the line or been hired since the strike. The anger at "scabs," people who had kept working during the strike, was savage. To the strikers, scabs were people who were stealing bread off their tables by doing their jobs and keeping Heartland running, undermining the power of the strike.

Then, on the last day possible, the strikers walked back in together and stood in the lobby, waiting to see what would happen. The current employees walked past them as they came in to work. Some stared and some dropped their eyes or turned away.

Lockout

The response of the Director was to lock them out. That is, she said no, they could not come back to work, they had to leave the premises. They stood there, in the sun coming through the big ornamental windows of the atrium, looking at the workers who had taken their places. The Director came and ordered them all to leave. By August, 2008, the workers were no longer technically on strike, they were on "lockout." That means that they had unconditionally offered to go back to work but had been refused.

They did not give up. They continued to picket and staff the strike hut, which was frequently vandalized and painted with obscene graffiti. This kept them visible in the community and especially to people coming in and out of Heartland. In the summer, large contingents of AFSCME members came down to Effingham in busloads and picketed. For a community that was famous for being white, if not actually Teutonic, the sudden presence of a big, loud crowd of racially diverse Chicago union activists was a shock.

During the lockout, the workers' strategies moved to another level and were extended in many directions. One strategy was to try to find another community health organization that would take over the workload from Heartland. Another was to appeal to the State of Illinois to stop funding an agency that was refusing to honor labor laws. The state in fact did an audit and discovered bad accounting and substantial amounts of missing money. The state then withheld some funding. All of this made news.

In November 2008, the Heartland workers received a visit from Richard Trumka, Secretary-Treasurer of the AFL-CIO. Trumka promised national publicity as the "poster child for

EFCA," the proposed Employee Free Choice Act. Were it made law, the EFCA would make a big difference for workers like those at Heartland. Instead of striking and being locked out without a contract, the law would mandate that at their first contract arbitration an arbitrator would demand that both sides agree to a contract. The contract signed under EFCA probably would have looked a lot like the one proposed by the mediator. However, this law was never brought to a vote in Congress as the Obama administration, facing a short timeline before the mid-term elections, instead put all its muscle into getting healthcare reform passed.

Finally, in the summer of 2009, nearly four years after the Director "dropped the bomb" that began this intense and drawn-out campaign, the relentless pressure by the union and the high visibility of the struggle in the Effingham community added the straw that broke the camel's back. The Board fired the Director and replaced her with a man who let it be known that he was willing to bargain.

Soon after that the new Board signed a contract with the union.

Back to work after four years

In early September, 2009, twenty of the original one hundred sixty workers went back to work. Some had moved away, some had taken other jobs, some had found other ways to scrape together a living. While some had had "the greatest experience of my life," others were burned out and suffering from stress.

The ones who did go back now had the difficult task of working side-by-side with people whom they had been calling "scabs" for the past two years. One woman could not forget the filthy words that had been spray-painted onto the strike hut walls. Now scabs and strikers met in the cafeteria. Who was going to make coffee for whom? Who was going to sit at a table with someone who had crossed the picket line? Who was going to teach the job to someone who had been doing it for a year but doing it wrong? The four years of struggle had divided the two groups not only by what they had done but by what they had learned. The workers who had been on strike had developed capabilities that brought them as a group to public attention on a state and even national level.

The vice-president for the union at Heartland was a young woman named Gail Warner. Gail had been the main public speaker after the union president Lucille Musser had taken ill. She had invested enormous amounts of energy in the strike. When she went back in, she found that her job had been split up into several jobs and in effect, no longer existed. She wrote me this message about the day they returned to work:

> To let you know how walking back into work went. I heard the local newscast as I drove in the parking lot at 7:30 a.m. and of course the lead story was about our return to work. I jotted down the exact words of the interim president of Heartland's Board for ya! It disgusted me.[He] said , "This is a sensitive process, we have a group of people who have been heroic in their efforts the past couple of years in terms of stepping up to make sure that clients of this community continued to receive the services they need and we owe them a great debt of gratitude." OF COURSE he was speaking about the scabs. It sickened me then and sickens me all over again to actually write it down.

> We entered the building, met all in one large room. Their HR person offered introductions, etc. and asked if we had any comments. ... The other

workers got to go into quiet rooms to take their online Essential Learning tests needed in order to return to work. I on the other hand was taken into the reception area, told to try and do my testing while working and I began working as if I had never left. It was odd! The scab I worked with seemed okay for two hours, then she told me to go to lunch; which I did, then when I returned from lunch, she lost her mind! She began to scream at me, curse at me and ultimately walked out. They offered her early layoff and she never came back. … I can elaborate on what was said sometime in person with you. Thursday and Friday went well, I haven't received much training, I just do the things I remember from 26 months ago and when something has changed (procedure wise) people pop in and tell me to change this or that. So, I think maybe the worst is over as far as "scab" altercations, but who knows. The Board will choose a Director by the end of the year, and if they choose someone similar to [the previous Director] nothing will change. I dearly hope they make a wiser decision or working at Heartland will be impossible for me. The whole need for our struggle was to make Heartland better, and if that doesn't happen, it will be difficult for me to watch it remain about money and power and not about helping people. Time will tell. Azure and I are going to Chicago to speak at the Labor Day event at Pullman. I will let you know how that goes as well. Gail

A few days later, Gail quit in order to spend time with her three-year old daughter. The stress of returning to work in that place was just too much.

Another union leader, Anna Beck, took over the VP position. In January 2010 she reported that the hardest thing about going back in was getting the management to agree that there actually was a contract in place and that they had to read it and acknowledge what it said, and that it would be a good idea for them to agree on what it said. Anna Beck had previous union experience. She knew what a grievance looked like, and what it meant to take something to arbitration, so she put a lot of energy into maintaining the union consciousness on the floor. But it was a different kind of place now.

Four years is a long, long time to be involved in a struggle. One of the remarkable things about this story is that the union, the Illinois State Council 31 of AFSCME, invested a tremendous amount of staff time and support. They rented an office in downtown Effingham and kept it staffed with at least one full-time staffer and a few part-time staffers. Regional director Jeff Bigelow made frequent visits. They trained the workers. They encouraged and supported things that the workers came up with. Real leaders emerged from among these workers. The union made these emerging leaders the face of the struggle and encouraged them to pass on their experience to workers in other struggles. To use terms from learning theory, they supported the creation of a *community of practice* and developed a participant structure that gave many of the strikers things to learn and real work to do.

When I asked Mike Newman, an AFSCME leader, why his union had been willing to spend so much money, staff time and political capital to back up this little group of mostly women at a private sector facility in deep Central Illinois, he smiled and said, "AFSCME has never lost a strike." Whether this is true of the whole national union or just of Illinois I don't know, but it is consistent with AFSCME's evaluation of the difficulties organizing at Effingham. It was far from being an obvious win.

When people have been through an organizing effort, especially one that is extremely painful and tears a town apart, they have learned something that stays with them for life. From the perspective of workers at other workplaces, the Heartland workers provide an example of success that sits there and doesn't go away. This becomes a problem for the town fathers. In the case of Effingham, while the town fathers were able to keep the brake lining company that would have paid $20 an hour away, it was going to be hard to get rid of these workers at Heartland, who were not likely to unlearn the lessons of their organizing.

Not that these lessons were all positive. What people take away from an experience is determined by how they interpret it. How they deal with the second, third and fourth stages of the learning cycle is very important. Not everyone who goes through experiences like "the bomb," the vote to form a union, the strike, or the vote to go back in and the lockout will interpret these events the same way. Not everyone will weigh the turmoil of the struggle against the protections of the contract and say it was worth it.

What did the struggle accomplish?

There are many ways to evaluate the results of the struggle at Heartland. They could be a list of friends lost or made, lives ruined or saved, fights, parties, enduring splits in the social world of the town, critical dates and deadlines. One way is, were these workers able to turn bad jobs into good ones?

This can be answered in part by looking at their contract. From a learning perspective, a contract is a map of a *participant structure,* a term that means different ways that people are enabled to participate in some activity. Paths pass through this structure. Some paths are dead ends, some create opportunities. When we are talking about a union contract, the activity would be the way that the union gives a voice and power to workers at that workplace.

There are two areas of the Heartland contract that speak to the question of whether these jobs are now better than they were before the struggle. Both have to do with the social relationships of work. Under this contract, the social relationships of work at Heartland have been changed.

The first change has to do with the relationship between the employer and the collectivity of workers, which is the union or the bargaining unit. The new contract says that work will be assigned to bargaining unit members who are already working at Heartland, not new people hired from outside. It also says that when someone new is hired, the union will be notified of it. And it gives the union ten days of paid time to send members to conferences and conventions.

The union gets to choose four stewards, who are allowed paid time to work on solving problems involving workers (grievances). The stewards will have access to a phone and a private meeting space, and the employer has to meet with them and work on the problems. If the steward and the employer can't work out a solution, then the grievance procedure moves on to mediation and ultimately arbitration, which is enforceable. This means that the union has a legitimate and substantial presence in the workplace. It can continue to build a *community of practice* on its own terms. There are also quarterly labor-management meetings, with five persons from each side to be in attendance. All these union rights establish a viable collective presence in the workplace that has the explicit purpose of protecting and advocating for the workers.

The second area has to do with the relationship between the employer and individual workers. The most familiar and standard one is seniority. Assignments, whether to working overtime, working on holidays, asking for paid time off, such as vacations, promotions, crisis line work or layoffs, are done by seniority or reverse seniority. This not only prevents favoritism, it acknowledges that workers learn while working, and that senior workers know something young workers don't know. Discipline, in the sense of punishment, is progressive under this contract, meaning that the punishments progress from mild to severe: an oral reprimand, a written reprimand, suspension, and then discharge. Progressive discipline is also supposed to be corrective, not punitive. It is supposed to teach, not intimidate. This shifts the balance of power between worker and management toward the center and reduces the role of fear and intimidation. Discipline can be grieved. The contract also explicitly says that discipline must be carried out "in a manner that will not embarrass the employee."

Part-time workers also received at least some of their health insurance payments back. There is, not accidentally, a no strike/no lockout clause, in effect for the duration of this contract. And they got a raise.

How do the workers feel? Did the struggle improve the jobs? Azure Newman said, "I think we're doing better than before. The turnover rate before the strike was enormous. It used to be that they'd make us sign a paper with the job description including the words 'at will.' Now, clients know we are going to be there. We have a job, we have protection." But look what it took to make it happen.

Gail wrote to me when a couple of years had passed:

> Working day and night, putting my reputation on the line, and walking a thin line where this town was concerned …I felt the pressure every day to just walk away and keep my mouth shut. I really didn't want to risk my husband's job (our only income), but in light of all the unfairness at Heartland I HAD to follow through and we HAD

to win for everyone involved. We did WIN, but I LOST in the end. I have moved on, but there will always be a rawness to the whole ordeal. I learned so much about my town and the people in it. I wouldn't trade the experience I gained in public speaking or the friends I made. It was sure a learning period in my life! and I am grateful for it. You do not need to print any of this, I just wanted to give you a better sense of how difficult it was, with management even using our own contract against us, to place a wedge in our solidarity, in our devotion to one another. They didn't succeed, but they did know how to rub salt into the wounds and it was a very difficult time. Oh, and the scab that screamed at me and quit, they later made her their "marketing manager"! They hired her back on when I left and she worked in a very high paying position there for years after I left. She eventually stepped out of line with the Director and she found out what they are really like and she walked out for good.

Azure Newman, one of the other stalwarts, is still at Heartland. She was offered a promotion to management in 2013 and took it, even though it meant she would lose the protection of the union. "It's been an interesting experience so far, to say the least," she says, "but then, that could be said of just about everything in my life over the past eight years."

Incidentally, I showed this chapter to the Heartland women who are quoted here and got their permission to use these quotes.

They say that knowledge is power, but that saying doesn't quite get at the truth. You can learn information that can be used against you, or in a way that you don't control. You can possess knowledge that gives other people power and leaves you weak. Knowledge is not power – organizing is power.

CHAPTER 8:
HOW CHILDREN LEARN ABOUT THEIR PARENTS' WORK

"I have seen a family rise from oblivion."
— Son of an AFSCME member

This chapter presents stories that can be looked at as descriptions of a *community of practice*. In this case, the *community of practice* is the union, but it extends beyond the regular membership of the union and includes the families of union members. The children have a legitimate presence in this community because they depend on the outcomes of union struggles and can support and even participate in these struggles. The sons and daughters of union members observe their parents acting, learning, sometimes taking leadership roles in the union. Sometimes they even join their parents at work.

Viewing the sons and daughters of union members as legitimate participants in the union's community of practice changes how we normally answer the question, "Who belongs to the union?" The children of members are usually forgotten. But no one observes the behavior of parents as closely as children do.

Stories as a way to organize experience

Sometimes the best way to find out what someone knows is to ask them to tell you a story. The flow of narrative will take over and organize the sequence of events, summon up details. suggest cause and effect, bring things to a conclusion. As the storyteller creates the story, the listener can see the picture. A good storyteller can actually walk the listener around *Kolb's Learning Cycle*.

I quoted Jerome Bruner in Chapter 6, who said that stories provide "a map of possible roles and of possible worlds in which action, thought, and self-definition are permissible." The possible roles and possible worlds that these young people describe are unknown to the over 90% of the US workforce that has no union representation. In fact, if we look back to Chapter 3, we can see that some of the stories told by these young people contain the very "forbidden lessons" that many people never get a chance to learn. We need to think about what use is made of the knowledge these young people have.

The children of families that are on the edge financially have an added reason to pay close attention to how their parents handle their jobs. They see their parents worrying, figuring things out, trying, failing and succeeding. The outcome of each struggle will impact the children: will they keep their health insurance? Will they be able to go on vacation? Will the parent have to take the evening or night shift? The children are limited in what they can do to help. No matter how much they might want to, they can't contribute much to the solution of the family problems. When and if help comes, they pay attention. As the parents learn, the children watch the parents learn and absorb their own lessons.

For example, one girl described how when she was little she would get up to get ready for school and find her mother asleep on the couch in the living room, too tired to take off her shoes. The mother was working a day job *and* a night job. The girl remembers laying a blanket over her mother before leaving for school. This mother decided they should move to Florida to save money on heat. When the move didn't work out, they drove back up to New England and the mother went back to her old jobs.

Then somehow the mother found a union job. For the girl, it's as if she never really met her mother before. Her mother enjoyed a full night's sleep. She had weekends off. She came home from work every afternoon and cooked dinner. They were simple, normal things, but before the union job they sounded like fairy tales. Before, the mother was a like a ghost; now, they had a relationship. They could make plans. One of these days they'll take a vacation! And because they now have insurance, the girl is going to go see a dentist for the first time in her life.

This story doesn't tell us anything about the kind of work the mother does or what the union does in that workplace. It is much bigger than that. The girl learns who her mother is, what it's like to have a mother, what a normal life feels like. A change at work leads to a change in the life of a family. Years from now she will remember the union job as a turning point for her and her mother.

Where these stories come from

These stories come from a set of scholarship applications submitted every year to AFSCME, the same union that helped the workers in Effingham organize. The stories, which are one to six pages long, typically cover a span of about eight years, accounted for by the fact that the authors are eighteen-year-olds who probably started being aware of what their mothers or fathers did at work at about age ten. This arc of time gives these stories the weight and gravity of biography. The children are deeply proud of their parents. They love them. They hate to see them intimidated, scared, abused and disrespected, but they cannot act on their hate. In a way, the children are the ultimate advocates for their parents, but they are also powerless. All they can do is watch. Sometimes what they see is a crisis. Sometimes it's a brave act, when the parent takes up a challenge that was previously beyond their capability, faces down the boss, makes a speech at a rally, or runs for election. Good or bad, the child notices, thinks about it and comes to conclusions. The conclusions they come to are different from what they will learn in social studies at school or from the mainstream media. They learn a strike is a good way to get your point across, collective action can work, without a union workers are helpless, sacrifices must be made, fighting back makes people feel better, democracy matters, and sometimes things take a long time to work out.

The prompt for the scholarship application essay, "What does AFSCME mean to my family?" elicits stories that tell us how parents deal with hazardous work, problems getting the right tools, political interference from elected officials, retaliation for whistle-blowing, work-related injuries, stress and violence, discipline, speed-up, job actions and strikes, political campaigns organizing campaigns, and fear. Many, of course, talk about healthcare, because getting or losing a job that provides access to healthcare can be a matter of life or death.

The union is in the picture, but it doesn't do magic. The crises that these young people describe may work out over the course of months or years. It may take three years for a worker to get her job back after being unfairly discharged.

Taken individually, these essays are emotionally gripping to read. Together, they form an annual portrait of this public sector workforce that does not exist in any other place. As pure research, this portrait would be unthinkably expensive if not impossible to reproduce. Added to that is the fact that it comes from the standpoint of the sons and daughters of workers who have working class jobs with "middle class" incomes, at a time when economic pressure on that workforce has been intensifying. Jobs are eliminated, workloads escalate, and in some states public sector workers are directly attacked by the legislators in the very governments that employ them. These are people doing tough jobs that involve lots of interpersonal psychological effort. They take place in prisons, welfare offices, police departments, hospitals, highways and schools. Their children see it all.

Why young people write these essays

Three characteristics of these essays are noteworthy. One is that these young people are writing to a prompt that predisposes them to express their view of their parent's union positively. Another is that the writers are self-selected by access to information about these scholarships. Not every local of this national organization gets equally good information about how to apply. Third, these are high school students who expect to go to college and can manage the deadlines for the various documents, including this application, that go with a college application. These factors shape the essays. Young people whose parents have had a bad experience with the union, or who never hear about these scholarships or can't deal with deadlines, do not write these essays.

The AFSCME Family Scholarships are substantial enough -- $2,000 per year for four years – so that hundreds of high school seniors complete these applications every year. They have to include a cover sheet verifying the parent or guardian's membership, letters of recommendation, test scores, grade transcripts and the essay. The most important part is the essay. The whole package is a complex three-way evaluation of the letters, scores and grades. The essay readers not only judge the student, they also judge the parents and the parent's local union.

For six years I was a member of the committee that judges these applications. With my research assistants, Jocelyn Graf, Karen Ford, and our program secretary Nancy Lahare, we read over 4,000 essays. For this chapter, I randomly chose 250 applications from the years 2005 and 2006. From these I took the 84 that had the signature of the applicant agreeing to the following condition: "All essays written as part of the application process for this scholarship competition become the property of AFSCME... I agree that AFSCME may identify me as the author of my essay if it decides to reprint, describe or excerpt my essay in publications other than Public Employee magazine."

Stress, pride and respect

Many of the stories talk about how stress at work puts stress on the whole family:

> The union came to us at a time when my mother needed someone to slay her dragons. ... When my mother first started working, her bosses could manipulate things for their advantage and make decisions at whim. By coming home frustrated and stressed, my mother often made us stressed and anxious. Now my mother's interests are represented... My brother and I do not worry that my mother would not be able to come pick us up from school if we get sick because she does not have to argue in order to leave work early.... My mother is much less stressed than she was in her early days of working without a union... without it, the dragons would definitely devour my mother and break our hearts.

The young people take pride in their parent's pride in their work:

> My dad, especially, has had to work jobs that he hated and that did not give him everything he deserved. He stuck it out until he found the one job that we all could count on. ...also a big part of having the township job is being proud of it. My dad doesn't have to be embarrassed of his employment any more.

Respect is often the trigger issue that leads someone to the union:

> My mom, a teacher's aide...had never worked in a job supported by a union before...most recently her own job and pay were negatively affected by administrative decisions at the school. My mom and other teacher aides were very upset and felt de-valued as employees by this. They went to the union representative who held several meetings with the aides. Union representatives listened to their concerns and gave experienced advice to the aides. After several discussions and a vote, the union representatives brokered a deal with the administration that not only gave them their salary adjustment back, but got their deal sweetened with some extras. My mom was exhilarated....

One applicant, after describing how her shy mother had learned to be much more assertive because of her active participation in the union, wrote:

> I went to the rally that my mother wanted to go to, and it turned out that she was up on the platform, speaking. I was so proud of her that I started to cry.

Another girl was worried when her mother started to get more involved in the union:

> It turns out that it was not so great. Our family life became more unusual than ever; our phone was ringing off the hook every single hour of the day. My mother's pager constantly buzzed

and she was stopped in supermarkets by other employees to ask her questions or advice on a problem that they had. I was embarrassed beyond belief because my mother speaks English but not very well. Her verb tenses were off and she would mix up nouns and adjectives when speaking to her fellow employees...(But she] is an example of someone who always pursued her dreams. She is an immigrant who overcame poverty to come to the United States and thirty years later, she is a successful labor leader who is an advocate for patients and nurses. She is a model citizen for immigrant nurses to speak up on issues and working conditions that need to be addressed. ...

Fear of danger

Other stories are about the physical danger their parents are exposed to at work:

When I was around the age of five, my father got a call on Christmas Eve, and the crew needed him out immediately to help clear the roads in one of the most violent snow storms Indiana County had ever seen. I was terrified and my mother was as well.

It's not just the weather:

As an Equipment Operator II, my father must operate a semi-truck and trailer rig in sometimes hazardous conditions of ice and snow to deliver about 95,000 pounds of food and equipment to different prisons in the state. Sometimes he has been stuck out on the road for three days or more because of the weather. He is also required to work side by side with inmates in the warehouse when he is operating the loading equipment before and after deliveries...

Prison guards are represented by AFSCME in some states, and in some communities, those are the only jobs for miles around. Young people talk about mothers working as prison guards, looking to the union to keep staffing levels high enough for safety.

Sometimes the threat is political:

AFSCME has given my father a method of defense to use when elected officials have attempted to push through their own agenda, not necessarily with the best interest of the City in mind. When my father has stuck with following ordinances, he has had his job threatened. However, due to his membership in AFSCME, they cannot fire him without just cause. Being in AFSCME grants my father the security to not be afraid of politicians and their agendas, where someone not in AFSCME would fear of his/her own job security. AFSCME allows my father to do his job to the best of his ability, instead of having to bow to the view of politicians.

The moment of crisis

Many stories begin with a crisis. A worker who thinks he or she has job security finds out there is none. This is the old question again: *"Can they do that?"* Sometimes the answer comes as a complete surprise.

> [My mother] went to work one afternoon in June 1995 after being harassed by her supervisor for two years. She was told that particular day she was no longer eligible to be an employee. She was downsized out of her position because she was making the most money in her position and new people could be hired for minimum wage. Due to no union protection, she was forced to become unemployed...

This boy notes the actual moment when he understood that employers and workers have different ultimate self-interests:

> My father started working for the Department of Corrections in 1999... At that time, I began to develop a better understanding of what unions are for and their purposes. I came to realize that you won't get ahead and be able to take care of your family by just showing up to work and giving the company 100% of your efforts without the unions backing you up...

Democracy and meetings

The sight of actual democracy in practice can be a revelation:

> I have been to a union meeting first hand and have witnessed people raising their hands with questions, laying their concerns out on the table, and voting on significant issues that affect them and their families.

So is the power of a collective response:

> ...From the time I was two until age nine, my mother was often away from the house, attending

union meetings. My brother and I would often accompany her to these meetings, carting our fast-food bags and whatever new plaything that came with it. The meetings consisted of loud and large words I didn't understand….One meeting in particular lies imprinted in my memory forever. A man was bellowing loudly at my mother. In an instant she had the entire conference room behind her, at her defense. …That night I felt ethereally lifted to a greater sense of realization as to what it means to be a human and interact with others. I was profoundly proud of my mother, and in awe that she had made such infallible connections with the people in her union. … I recently learned that while I was admiring her friendships and character, she organized the first ever AFSCME at the University of Minnesota…and helped break a ten-year string of wage freezes.

With the power of collective activity behind you, you are "equal with management." The answer to "Can they do that?" is no longer an automatic "Yes":

My mother has been on the committee that sits down and works on the agreement known as a "union contract" to the bargaining unit. They sit at the bargaining table as equals with management… My mother is a union Shop Steward who organized the employees in her shop, convincing them to join the AFSCME Union in 1998. I have accompanied her to lots of her shop steward meetings. My mom's dedication is even felt in our home where she discusses union laws and regulations with some of the employees she represents. While home on the telephone she constantly reminds them of how on the job they get protection of a contract and more strength in the workplace.

Pushback

While the greatest stress and anxiety comes from the fear of job loss, the most positive emotional stories are about pushing back through collective action. The pushback can be meeting with the boss, filing a grievance, engaging in civil disobedience, negotiating a contract or going on strike. On the surface, this seems like a contradiction. If people are afraid to lose their jobs, shouldn't they feel even more scared to push back? The young people don't think so. In fact, the opposite appears to be true. Stories of struggle are told with glee:

> Dinner time in my house is a time for the family to get together....my father is a "waste manager" for the city of XXX but we all know him as Trash-Man. As shop steward....we get to break in on the "wheelings and dealings" between [his fellow workers and management] each vying for the maximum benefits... These dinner sessions have been important lessons in life, learning that people have different perspectives on things...shaping how we interact with each other and whether or not we can successfully cohabitate...As recent as last summer contract negotiations for my father's job and the jobs of his band of trash collecting forces, were in limbo... I have never seen my father so worried. Keeping his job was top priority and of course, cutting costs is always a priority of an employer, so the struggle to keep jobs along with the benefits and perks we had grown used to

was a balancing act the Ringling Brothers would have trouble keeping up. In the end, the contracts were renewed, dramatic envisions of food stamps were put to an end....The things most others wouldn't see I have been given the opportunity to contemplate...

The writer uses strong words ("limbo", "worried," "struggle," "dramatic"). We gather that this learning experience, for the son as well as the father, is infused with strong emotion. At the same time, the grasp of what is going on ("wheelings and dealings," "people have different perspectives on things") is broad and the experience is collective ("my father's job and the jobs of his band of trash-collecting forces"). In the end, "the contracts were renewed," which is a win, although the writer doesn't bother to say that. "Winning" doesn't mean punishment, revenge or crushing the opposition. It means that life is back to normal, the way things are supposed to be.

This one is more straightforward about winning:

> ... I have witnessed the good that union victories have on the morale of a family first hand...I have also seen this firsthand through my brother who has had to file grievances against the administration. The zeal at which his problems went away.. was incredible. The threat was there that put the power into the hands of the underdog, who was backed by the union. ... I have seen a family rise from oblivion to a state of comfort they never knew before.

> January 26th was the day that taught me the true definition of fear...The day my father was wrongfully terminated was the first day in my

life that I thought I might lose him. Knowing that he had done nothing wrong, he stood on his honesty and faith and chose to stand up for himself, with the backing of his local, district and state representatives of AFSCME...What terrified me the most was that because he did not have a job to support us, he would just give up. Boy was I wrong! [The] president of our local union, came to the rescue...After many attempts to settle this dispute on the local level, we were left no choice, it was time for arbitration. [They] prepared my father for his day in court. They prepared all of our witnesses and evidence and made sure they were fully prepared to face this battle...What I did not realize was for the next four months we would be forced to wait and see if our efforts would pay off. November 13, 2000, was the day that my dreams came true. We had won! My father was found completely innocent. ...AFSCME taught me to have faith and hope that the innocent will be justified....

Strikes as a good experience

Strikes, in these stories, are not crises in and of themselves. The reason for the strike is a crisis, but the strike itself is not. Sometimes you hear people say, "No one wants to go on strike." This is clearly not always true. These young people generally take strikes to be a sign of strength and hope, an opportunity to exercise their rights and experience solidarity:

During the AFSCME Council 6 strike in 1999 the union helped to protect my mother's job position, status and wage while my mom proudly walked the picket line. When the strike was over she still had a job to go back to and our family still retained the benefits which helped to keep our medical bills down and our family out of debt. Also my mom was able to teach me a valuable lesson in standing up for what I believe in. By walking the picket line, even when other people don't agree with her, she has shown me that I am entitled to my beliefs...

Another strike story:

The local union decided to strike because of health care and wage issues. Both my parents walked off their jobs to show support...my stepfather would go from his chemotherapy treatments to walk the picket line and my mother was also walking the picket line as well as working part time to assist our family since both of their paychecks would cease [during the strike]. My stepfather felt weak and tired and if the strike were to last too long they would have to pay for the premiums of the insurance. Each chemo treatment was $1,000... The president of the local learned of their situation and stated that the union would stand behind my parents 100% of the way [e.g., would pay their premiums] ...."Crossing the picket line" was definitely not an option for my parents...

These young people understand the disciplined choreography of a well-run strike. Strikes are hard work and take just as much organizing and planning as going to your regular work:

My dad has been involved in 2 strikes for the Department of Human Services of the last few years. Even though I don't live with my dad, I still could feel the impact of the strike. I knew that when the strike was going on, that even though he was not getting paid, he was fighting for what he felt would benefit his family in the long run. The work and effort that is involved in the strike is a lot like you are working. He still got up in the morning and got ready for work just like any other day. You try to schedule who is going to be where, and when. You stand out in the cold and rainy weather and carrying signs, showing what it is that you are fighting for. All this was so that my dad and all the other AFCSME members would get the pay that they deserve, and the benefits that are so valuable to all the families.

These young people are learning about work, but not learning the traditional job skills which is the content of most job training programs. Although their parents maintain public buildings, serve public aid clients, process convicted felons into prison and run government offices, that is not what they are learning, either. They are learning the kind of knowledge that this book is being written to describe.

- It is *strategic knowledge*: how to keep a job, how to do the work safely, how to resist intimidation, how to manage an excessive workload, how to negotiate a decent wage.
- It is *specific* to the social relationships, economic and legal, at a particular moment in *history*.
- It is *collective*: these strategies are not something that individuals carry out alone. They require a sense of how an individual belongs to a whole class of people who are similarly situated. It involves knowing whom to trust and where the real lines of authority flow.

This type of learning cuts across all kinds of work, whether one is a cafeteria worker, a civil engineer, a home care worker or a park manager. It is being learned in a context of worry, sleepless nights, fear, and sometimes relief, triumph and pride – strong emotions, which in turn shape the learning itself.

Working alongside a parent

How far do the young people really enter into the community of practice? Do they get past the dinner table conversations and find out about the actual workplace? In some cases, yes. The sons and daughters not only attend union meetings, conventions, parades and picnics, they also volunteer at their parent's workplaces and share their parent's work experience:

> Another benefit of my mom getting a job at the veterans' home is that I have found myself volunteering much more often. ... I mostly keep the members entertained during their spare time. For example, I played guitar for a blind member at the home who loved music. A member who had lost an arm and both of his legs had many talks with me about the dangers of alcohol and drugs, but he also talked to me about his point of view on hate...One Sunday morning right after lunch we had a long conversation about hate. During this conversation he told me, "Hate is baggage. Nothing comes from hate except violence. And violence only causes more hate."

Another said:

> I have volunteered at The Manor, the nursing home where my mother works, for the past six years. I have seen a lot of changes mostly good

because of the union. ...Through the years of my volunteering, I have seen many tears from workers and even from my mother for the way they were treated by the management. Most of it was unfair discipline practices usually followed with suspension or even worse, termination... Many times employees would be in trouble because they had called in sick for themselves or family members...

More often than one might expect, they engage in paid, part-time work alongside their parents:

For the past four years of high school I have been hired to help my mother set up her breakfast room. I have to get up at 5:30 every morning to make it to school so I can help set up...[this schedule] makes it unable for her to sleep past 5 am and I have always wondered why she never switched to a different career earlier in life since the times were so harsh.

These young people write as if they feel part of something. First and foremost they are part of their family. But at the same time they are acutely aware of how much their families depend on the union for everything, from being able to count on seeing their mother at dinner, to the safety standards keeping her from injury, to paying for dental work. When union actions take place outside the workplace, like on a picket line or a union meeting or celebration, they join in. They support their parents by taking care of their siblings when necessary. They should be considered part of the overall *community of practice.*

The story of the strike, above, makes a good test of this idea. When these children describe a strike, are they describing a community of practice? How do they see their participation? We can draw up a table to try to match the theoretical conditions for learning against quotes from the stories about a strike.

Looking at this table, you can see what would be lost if a parent tried to conceal the fact that he or she was going on strike or kept the economic risks and consequences of the strike secret from the family.

From the point of view of these children, strikes are seen as honorable, orderly and legitimate activities. They are seen as an opportunity to clarify what is important. What it is you are fighting for, as Lave put it. They are very much a collective, rather than individual activity. People are engaged "for substantial periods of time, day by day, in doing things in which their ongoing activities are interdependent." (Lave) Sometimes the children join their parents on the picket line, sometimes they just hear about it. Either way, they have a good grasp of what is going on and why. *(Please see Table 2 pp 130-31)*

What use is made of this learning?

So what happens next? What is done with this learning? This knowledge? If the strike takes place in a school, do the young people come back to class and write about what they have learned? If the teachers have won a good contract, do the students study the contract and build their math assignments on costing out the wage and benefit provisions?

Probably not. This is usually another situation in which hard-won knowledge about the social relations of work in the US lies on a shelf and fades into memory. Too many times, in fact, workers try to conceal challenges at work from their sons and daughters because they are afraid of making them anxious. Instead, these young people are proud to see their parents fighting back.

Table 2. Are the young people describing a community of practice?

Condition for learning	Quote from story	Does this satisfy a condition of what makes a community of practice?
Is the learning seen as legitimate by the total community of practice?	"..showing what it is you are fighting for..." "Also my mom was able to teach me a valuable lesson in standing up for what I believe in. By walking the picket line, even when other people don't agree with her, she has shown me that I am entitled to my beliefs..."	Yes: Strike is a product of the union decision, collectively undertaken.
Is the whole process visible and transparent to the participant?	"..a lot like you are working.." "You try to schedule who will be where and when..."	Yes: The strike activities have been standardized and communicated.
Is the learning process supported by the leadership?	"...The president of the local learned of their situation and stated that the union would stand behind my parents 100% of the way [e.g., would pay their premiums]"	Yes: Someone in authority arranges the schedule which is enacted collectively. Leadership publicly supports member effort.

Does the work done by learners have value to the community?	"...what it is you are fighting for... the pay that they deserve, and the benefits that are so valuable to all the families." "I knew that when the strike was going on, that even though he was not getting paid, he was fighting for what he felt would benefit his family in the long run."	Yes. This is a struggle over essential benefits. The success of the strike depends on the ability of the membership to carry it out. Families know about what is going on and support it and will be ready to support future efforts, too.

A lesson for unions

One of the things a *community of practice* is supposed to be able to do is perpetuate itself by passing its power and strength on to the next set of activists. The theory in which we look at learning as taking place in a community of practice contains a severe warning, something many unions find difficult: how to build on the learning that takes place during a period of mobilization, and how to find leadership opportunities for people who during the mobilization showed that they are leaders. Just as the unionized journeymen in the next chapter have to be conscious that the slow, clumsy, nervous apprentices who follow them around on the job are actually the same workers who are going to be paying into their future pensions and governing their union, so the leaders who have put their members and their families through a strike have to be conscious that among these foot soldiers, including the young people, are the next generation that has to be ready to step in when the older generation is gone.

Consciousness is not enough, however. Consciousness has to motivate a deliberate strategy accompanied by structure and a dedication of resources. If the positions of leadership are going to be something more than just a job for the incumbents, the rungs of the ladder have to be full of climbers and the hallways of the community of practice have to be full of aspiring practitioners.

In the communities of practice that Lave and Wenger studied, this structure was sometimes explicitly organized and resourced, sometimes weak, and sometimes absent. When it is weak, communities die slowly; when it is absent, they are just a flash in the pan.

CHAPTER 9:
CONSTRUCTION INDUSTRY APPRENTICESHIPS AS COMMUNITIES OF PRACTICE

In the middle of my life
I found myself
In a dark wood
where the path was not easy to see...
— Dante Alighieri, *The Divine Comedy*

This chapter is about a community of practice that is defined by an economic agreement: the agreement in the unionized construction industry and the unions that train apprentices. From the employer's point of view, the training of apprentices, and their development into skilled journeymen, makes possible the perpetuation of a skilled workforce they can count on. From the union's point of view, the upcoming generation of new tradesmen needs to be well-trained in order to get hired and to pay into the retirement funds of older, retiring journeymen. The common interest in this community of practice is money.

This chapter will also raise issues about race and gender. The way race shaped the experience of the men in this chapter stands out so starkly that you might ask why look for any other lessons in these stories. Race and gender discrimination were indeed the issues that originally triggered the work that I describe here. All the men in the first group were African American. Half of the second group were African American, too. All our interviewees were men. Of the journeymen who helped with the interviews, three were African American and one was white.

However, all the men in both groups were trying to learn their chosen trade. That is what I am going to focus on. These settings illustrate the importance of meeting the essential measures of a *community of practice* if you want to develop the next generation of your community. When you read about the two settings, think about the characteristics of a good *community of practice*. Are they present? Is the path that takes someone from novice to expert clear, transparent, and known? Does the path they are following have acknowledged legitimacy? Does the newcomer feel he has a right to be there? Is he given real work to do, or is he shunted off into doing something irrelevant or repetitive? Do people who are learning get mentored? Do they get the supportive attention of someone who is more expert? The examples from the first group show what happens if the answer to these questions is "No." Some of the men who were interviewed were on the verge of despair, some harbored ill-concealed anger, and another one, who had been successful, attributed his success to luck and miracles.

Ideally, our national workforce development system was designed to provide a "seamless" labor market where workers with skills meet employers with jobs. This has not come to pass.

What apprenticeships do

Learning in an apprenticeship depends on getting the attention of other people who are more experienced and more expert than you are. This is especially important in construction. A certain amount of a trade can be learned by studying and taking classes, but, because building trades skills are so physical, like dance or cooking, they are best communicated by demonstration and practice. By working closely with someone else you learn the rhythm, the intensity, the beat of the work. (This should remind you of the Vygotskian idea of learning from a more expert peer.) You learn how to be part of a large team, sometimes involving hundreds of people. You learn how to fit in, how to make yourself useful. If you are useful, they will teach you more. This is what an apprenticeship is. It is also a tricky, close, personal relationship upon which a whole life's opportunities are riding. A good apprenticeship, in other words, is also a community of practice.

Formal apprenticeships

It is important to understand what a formal apprenticeship in construction looks like. It is a three to five year, 4,000-6,000 hour sequence in which apprentices take classes and do on-the-job (OJT) training. In construction, at least in the US, formal apprenticeships are actually regulated by a federal law, the Fitzgerald Act of 1935. That law was passed to create oversight of the use of apprentices in a period when child labor was not a distant memory. The law sets up what the program is supposed to look like, who pays for it, how much and how long people study, what they get paid, etc.

When Jean Lave and Etienne Wenger wrote their book, *Situated Learning,* they did not use any of the major formal construction apprenticeship programs as their examples. One of their examples might have been a formal apprenticeship, but it isn't clear because they don't describe it enough. Furthermore, their example was clearly a bad apprenticeship. It was in a butcher shop of a supermarket, where apprentices were relegated to wrapping meat and never learned how to actually cut it. It did not satisfy the requirements of a good community of practice.

Applying to a formal apprenticeship program is as complicated as applying to college. Some are as selective as the Ivy League. There are rules, forms to fill out, fees to pay, interviews and tests to pass. Apprentices are paid at a lower rate than journeymen, which makes them cheaper for the employer, but they also don't work as fast or as skillfully, which may make them more expensive. The number of apprentices accepted also depends on the need for workers with that level of skill, which in turn depends on how much construction activity is going on. If a lot of workers are needed, the waiting lists for apprenticeship slots move fast. If work is slow, getting in can take years. During the long waits between steps in the process, applicants can get lost. It helps if you have a father or an uncle in the trade who can guide you through this process. This is also known as "the sons and nephews problem," because access to some of the trades, especially in the past, has appeared to be something you inherit. In different cities, the trades have been historically dominated by certain ethnic groups, especially Germans and Irish. Lawsuits and regulations have tried to open up access, but with limited success.

The interviews

This chapter draws on two sets of interviews. My colleague Karen Ford did the first set of interviews in Chicago in 2003.

The men she interviewed had graduated from a pre-apprenticeship program called Building Bridges. Building Bridges targeted the "hard-to-employ." That means members of minority groups, ex-offenders, ex-addicts, men in their thirties, forties and sometimes fifties. Our charge was to provide our students with the basics they would need to apply to a full apprenticeship program. The classes met once a week for eleven weeks in church basements. We had very limited funds to work with. All the teachers were volunteers. We recruited through a network of African-American pastors on the south side of Chicago. Our umbrella organization, the Chicago Interfaith Committee on Worker Issues, was directed by the Rev. Anthony Haynes, himself an African-American pastor.

Although they were labeled "hard to employ," these men desperately wanted and needed work, not just because they needed to earn money. One man told me that he needed a job "in order to feel human."

A generation ago there would have been jobs for these men in manufacturing. By the early 2000s, those jobs had gone. Since welfare "reform" had kicked in, there was no general assistance for non-disabled men and very little welfare assistance for women and children. We recruited participants from communities where almost no money circulated. Things that had value were car parts and social security numbers. The possibility of a job in the unionized trades seemed like a ticket to heaven.

The Building Bridges curriculum was mostly math, some interviewing skills and at least one session on workers' rights. We also took students on a tour of different apprenticeship programs, typically Carpenters, Electricians and Bricklayers.

The guest speakers from the trades who talked to the students focused on preparing students to handle tough situations. One black Carpenter told how a white teacher had put a noose around a black apprentice's neck. When the apprentice reacted by hitting the white teacher, the apprentice was kicked out of the program. The lesson here was "to watch yourself and not let anyone make you do something that would take you out of the program." Another one, a black electrician who had become a Vice-President of his union, told a Building Bridges class that they would have to "put on armor every day" to keep from reacting angrily to insults at work.

While we had contacts with the United Brotherhood of Carpenters (UBC), the Laborers, the Bricklayers and the Electricians, most of the apprenticeship openings were with the Carpenters. However, not everyone wanted to be a carpenter, and we could not guarantee anyone a slot in an apprenticeship program. After they graduated we helped them apply, gave them some names and phone numbers and left it up to them to find their way.

The first three graduates whose interviews I will quote here were chosen to illustrate just how hard it is to see the paths they were trying to follow. Despite the boost our program had given them, they did not have the right set of resources to get access to a program that would train them. Desperate as they were for work, they couldn't find the path.

I want to mention that some of our graduates did get into formal apprenticeship programs. Even those, however, had to survive the months of waiting as the application process ground along.

"I'm working on it"

The interviews were done a year after most of the interviewees had graduated, meaning that they had been looking for work or had been waiting to hear from various apprenticeship programs for at least a year. This is not unusual; applying to an apprenticeship program can take as long as applying to a college.

Here is one man, 34 years old, talking about what he did when he finished the Building Bridges classes. Lacking a car or bus fare, he walked up and down the city streets, stopping wherever there was construction going on and asking about work.

> I go out every day. I go walking around to construction sites, asking around at places where they're doing work, like doing rehabbing. I tell them what I'm doing, looking to be an apprentice, and ask if I can come in and see what they're doing.
>
> After I finished the program I went to the location of the bricklayers and cement masons and found out that before we start (the application process)

there is a $20 fee to take the test. I didn't have this fee. I also didn't have reliable transportation. I am working on trying to get it. I am working on trying to get a car and my license. I also have this child support thing going on.

Couple days a week, I go to this place at 58th and Peoria. This man, I've known him for years. He knew my father. He said I could come and he'd tell me about what I will be doing. He shows me what to do, how to lay the bricks, how to set the mortar. He tells me what a foreman might ask me to do. I go up there two days a week for a couple of hours and he tells me what I need to know so that I'll know what I'm doing when I get into the apprenticeship program. He don't want to let me work there – it's a union site, I think, and he don't want to take the chance.

Behind the statement "he don't want to let me work there" is a story. If it's a union site, the union has the right to require that all the workers be union members and maybe even come from the union hiring hall. The union could file a grievance against the contractor if this foreman is seen letting someone off the street do some work. It wasn't just that this newcomer didn't have a right to be there. His presence was actually a violation of a contract. The relationship between him and the foreman was covert, not part of a transparent, legitimate process. Anything he learned might even carry, psychologically speaking, the shadow of being something stolen or obtained in secret.

He continued to describe his situation with a combination of optimism and frustration. Transportation, especially for inner-city residents who use buses and trains, don't have cars and don't even have drivers' licenses, is a major hurdle.

> A car would cost not really much. Someone I know got a car for $400. The most I will have to get is $1,000. I'll take the driver's license test on Tuesday. They won't take a State ID. You have to show a driver's license. You really have to have reliable transportation. Certain people, they might want to send me somewhere that's way out, you can't take the bus. Or they want to have me somewhere in twenty minutes, I need you at a certain time, you can't spend an hour on the bus.

Another reason that he can't use public transportation is that if the job site is out in the suburbs, which are relatively white, a black man walking down a street from the bus stop early in the morning is likely to attract police attention.

Nonetheless, he's not giving up:

> I'm going out every day trying to find something. It's going to work. I've just got to keep doing. I'm not quitting.

If you saw this man on the street, depending on who you are, it might not be easy to tell what he was doing. He might seem to be just wandering aimlessly, or hanging around construction sites with the intent to steal something. To appreciate the determination in his voice when he said, "I've just got to keep doing," imagine this scene: in the Building Bridges offices, when we gave practice math tests, many of our students would take the tests with one hand on their Bible. To "keep doing" is like a prayer.

"I got vast experience in a lot of everything."

Another man wanted to apply to the Painting and

Decorating Joint Apprenticeship program. He had applied to the Carpenters, but when he took the test to get into their apprenticeship program he failed the math section. It was timed, and he said he had never taken a timed test before and got rattled. He assumed that doing the work of a painter/decorator would involve less math and less measurement. However, the Painters and Decorators (International Union of Painters and Allied Trades, or IUPAT) application involved $500 in fees plus an intent-to-hire letter from a contractor. For this man, the $500 was an insurmountable problem. This man spoke to our interviewer, Karen Ford, as if she might have access to that $500:

> I say, let me go head on and do this. Like I said, I'm 50 years old and I need a job. Shoot, I'm trying to pay for a house here. You know, I got grandkids. Beaucoup responsibilities and I need a job like yesterday, you know. I got vast experience in a lot of everything. Like I say, decorating, I got a lot of experience in decorating. I got a lot of experience in plumbing. I got a lot of experience in carpentry, you know. But like I say, I ran into this obstacle with the Carpenters with failing the test.

Then he went to the Painters and Decorators union hall, where he met someone who had passed their test and was still waiting a year later to get into school. Now he is confused:

> The guy said, well, it's been over a year and I passed the test and I'm still waiting to get into school. Not work but to get into school! So I say wait, I ain't got another two to three years to be on the waiting list, you know, so I'm blessed that I have my health and strength. There's nothing wrong with me. I can give another ten years. I

think I got another good ten years in me, see what I'm saying? And I need to get started, you know what I'm saying. I need a job and I need to get started. I've had jobs before, machine operator, off and on jobs, little off and on jobs. I need something I can stay on, something I can latch onto for the next 10-15 years. That's why I say I got to sit down and find out how to get $500.

Industries come and go, but people need work

One man, the father of three children, was in his mid-forties. He had run through several of the "tech" industries as they came and went.

> In the Air Force I was a cable splicer and I got really interested in doing that kind of work. I started working with a cable TV back here in Chicago in 1984. I was with the first company that had cable. I was one of the first installers. I was with them from 1984 to 1998 and then moved on to RCN Telecommunications Corporation and got exposed to fiber optics. I was with them from 1998 to 2001 and got laid off. That was the year I got involved with you people [the Building Bridges Project]. I wanted to be in a trade, to be more self-sufficient.

After completing the Building Bridges Program he applied to the Electricians, the Plumbers and the Laborers apprenticeship programs. The Laborers accepted him into a two-week training program that gave him some safety and CPR certifications. This was not a full apprenticeship program. It just got him certified to do relatively unskilled labor on big sites. He described what they learned to do:

They had us using shovels, digging an area of certain dimensions as a group. We had to use wheelbarrows doing other things like simulating cement grading. We carried cement blocks and concrete forms from one place to another on uneven terrain.

After the two week training, he waited. Finally, the apprenticeship coordinator called him for a construction job. He went to the site.

The job lasted three days, very heavy physical work in a project that was already behind. I was giving myself maybe about a week to adjust. You know, maybe if I was 10 or 15 years younger, it might not have took a physical toll. But I was hurting after that first day. The foreman made a comment, "Man, what's wrong with your feet?" You know I got flat feet. If I'm on my feet for an extended period of time, I hurt bad. On that first day I could barely walk from that car to the door. But I was determined. Man, I got to do what I got to do. Hoping, man, just work with me. I'll be all right tomorrow. So Wednesday while I'm working he hands me a check and says we got to let you go. Tell them lack of work. We're going to have to pull all the apprentices off this job. That's what I was told.

I still got scars from lifting that stuff. I had dropped one of them on this finger. This whole finger was purple but I didn't report that cuz I need to support my family here. I was just giving myself a week or so to adjust to this type of work.

In the meantime, his wife was supporting the family as a cosmetologist.

Stories like this can be so breathtakingly bleak that you might ask, "What has learning got to do with this?" If these men are learning (and they are), what are they learning? Imagine mapping this man's experience onto *Kolb's Learning Cycle*. What he learned would be a whole world view of broken promises and harsh realities.

The path to getting a good job in construction, if you don't have the resources and connections to put your feet onto the bottom rung of the ladder, is so dark and uncertain that people trying to find it on their own may end up falling into despair, looking for a hustle or praying for a miracle.

"Everything is a miracle"

One man whom we interviewed had a story with a happy ending. He was only the seventh African American in union history to become a millwright with a turbine engine qualification. This is a very high-skill specialty within the Carpenters Union. This man was the son of a retired Air Force officer, had been in the Air Force himself, then worked in shipyards and in a power plant in the south. He came to Illinois to "step in" as he put it, during a famous strike at Caterpillar and stayed in Chicago when he was laid off after the strike was over. There is a long history, of course, of employers using African American workers as strikebreakers as a way of infusing a labor struggle with a racial dimension.

After he graduated from Building Bridges, he took the apprenticeship tests, did well, and got into the apprenticeship program. During breaks, he wandered down the hall and introduced himself to the instructor of the millwright's class who gave him some advice. In other words, he assembled a network for himself. Later, personal connections, this time at the union, got him connected with the millwrights and even sent to Las Vegas for special training in turbine engines. To him, this was a miracle. He said:

> I was just absolutely blessed, really blessed, and I feel that I have a connection with the Creator. I think that has a great deal to do with it. And you know the Creator puts me at the right place at the right time to meet the right people. I'm straight, honest and open, then the door continues to open. And that's what I am, always straightforward. How can I say it—a person with integrity. But you know when you get closer to the Creator, I mean really, really be a part of the Creator then you go through another process of understanding.

He links his feeling of being blessed with how he gets information:

> It's like being one with the Sustainer so you know you receive information in ways that you would probably not, linear. They come through dreams or maybe thinking about somebody's conversation when they're asking the question. And like, you're being still and you're listening and it comes. The process is right down the line. If you look at my situation it's like everything's a miracle. I'm probably the only Black certified turbine mechanic in Illinois. You know, some would say it's a miracle within itself that I'm in the millwrights. Because I'm the seventh Black in the millwrights. I'm the only Black with turbine qualification. And that sustains me so.

If something feels like a miracle to one man, it is not

something that is the norm for everyone. This means that it lacks the characteristics of a community of practice. This ladder was something that only this man could climb. In a community of practice, someone can move through a public, explicit sequence of ways to participate that legitimatize his or her participation and allow the whole ladder to be visible, all the way from newcomer to expert.

When Karen Ford was doing the interviews, she asked how the men originally found out about the Building Bridges Project. Their answers suggest both how accidental their contact was and how wide a range of experiences they came from:

- It was posted on the wall at the Chicago Christian Industrial League homeless shelter.

- I read about it in the Sun-Times.

- There was a flyer at the unemployment office.

- I heard about it through my church.

- I was working driving a cab and a co-worker had a flyer.

- When I was in jail, the guy told me about the apprenticeship program.

And what background knowledge did they have about unions? A little something, but not enough.

- My parents were in a union. They were teachers.

- Only thing I knew about a union was that they help you keep a job.

- I had no idea that that was a union right there. I thought it was a truck place.

- I rode past there plenty of times and never knew it was a school [a union apprenticeship program location].

- The union? I didn't know anything about no union.

A wrap-around community of practice, but short-lived

In the face of these experiences, the organizers of the Building Bridges Project could see what we needed. We were able to get a lot more funding. We designed what the participants called a "wrap-around program." In this new program, we had something much closer to a *community of practice:* both classroom and hands-on instruction, a weekly $200 stipend, bus passes, classes all day long five days a week for twelve weeks, and for each graduate, a set of tools and a pair of steel-toed boots. There were extra tutoring sessions for math and many chances to practice taking timed math quizzes. Then we provided counseling until they took the Carpenters apprenticeship entrance test. All of them passed and all of them got into the Carpenters apprenticeship program.

That's right -- *all of them passed.* Even men who, at the beginning of the program, could not do simple fractions or long division.

However, the funding for this wrap-around program did not come about because we critiqued the lack of structure and support in our previous program. Instead, it came about because of aggressive lobbying and sometimes bitter debate in the state legislature about historic racial discrimination in the building trades. None of the people involved at the state level knew about our program or what had happened to our graduates. We just happened to have a proposal ready.

But that was 2008 and the economy crashed, wiping out the residential construction work that would have given our graduates jobs. Whole apprenticeship programs closed down. Senior union apprenticeship instructors went back to working with the tools and were glad to have any job at all. Reverend Haynes lost his job. With the Building Bridges Project gone and no one in the office or answering the phone, we lost track of our graduates.

Apprentices in OJT placements

The experience of the Building Bridges graduates can be contrasted with the experience of apprentices after they have been accepted into a full-scale apprenticeship program.

This second set of interviews comes from apprentices enrolled in the apprenticeship program of Chicago-based Local 134 of the International Brotherhood of Electrical Workers (IBEW). These men had passed through a rigorous selection process. They had done the waiting and wondering. They had achieved what the men in the first set of interviews were hoping for. They were mostly African American, but they were younger than the men in the first group, and fifty years after the Civil Rights Act of 1964 there are sufficient African American and minority workers in the building trades that some of these men were themselves sons and nephews. These interviews were done with the help of Mark Berchman, a journeyman Electrician, and Emanuel Blackwell, an African-American journeyman in the Insulators Union (Heat and Frost Insulators and Allied Workers).

The first year of the IBEW apprenticeship includes eleven weeks of classroom-based activities. The next two years include nine weeks each of classroom, with the rest being on the job training, or OJT, followed by one more week in the classroom for the fourth and fifth year apprentices. The classroom experience is like school. It is in the OJT where apprentices encounter what is intended to be an acculturation into a community of practice.

An apprentice compared what learning in the classroom was like with OJT:

> In the classroom, everything is set up. It's laid out in order. Everything is arranged, connected. It's the ideal situation. If you're pulling wire, you're only pulling one at a time. The wire is on a spindle, it's measured. In the classroom, you don't have to be discovered. The classroom is the foundation from the book standpoint. You see something in the field, you go back in the classroom and "Now I know why we're doing it that way." You will never be able to 100% duplicate what is going on out in the field, in the classroom. Out in the field, you don't know what you're going to see. You run into things nobody told you about. It's on a different scale. But it all comes together.

In the classroom, exercises are standardized so that each student can be monitored. The performance of the individual student is not masked by interactions with others. For the student who wants to be recognized for effort or competence, this is a benefit.

In the classroom, the conditions for legitimacy and transparency are clearly met. But classroom work is not "real work," necessary for an effective community of practice. In the field, where apprentices face opportunities to do real work, the legitimacy and transparency issues are more complicated.

When the apprentice crosses into OJT, the prepared classroom vanishes and is replaced by the complex and often dangerous worksite. Here, the attentive teacher is replaced by the hurrying journeyman whose attention must be captured. In this structured environment, the new apprentices have to earn their legitimacy, their right to be there as learners. The journeymen may make them jump through some hoops to get this attention. One apprentice told us:

> If you're a helper, and you work with two journeymen, they may say, "Go get me this, go get me that." You go, and when you come back, they've got some of the stuff done and you don't know how they got it done.

Other journeymen will be serious and creative teachers. One journeyman remembered that his journeyman actually demonstrated how to use a trowel:

> He showed me how to hold my hand, hold a trowel in my hand and what angle to put my hand and how to turn my wrist. He actually touched my hand and told me to hold it this way, and he glided my hand across.

The work of an apprentice is evaluated by journeymen on the job and if it is approved, may be rewarded with more teaching. If it is not approved, the apprentice may be punished by being excluded from other opportunities to learn. The issue of "legitimacy" gets tested. Does the apprentice have a legitimate right to learn? It depends. The exchange is good work (in the eyes of the journeyman) for opportunities to learn. Apprentices reported how they felt themselves evaluated:

> They do not ask you what your skill level is. They can spot someone who is fresh.

> They can see if you're a "mope," a "hack," a guy who is really not putting everything into his work, a person who takes no pride in his work.

They don't tell you "good job," but they let you know. It's a complement and criticism all in one sitting. I like you and I like the work you're doing and we're going to teach you more.

If they don't like you, trust me, you will feel as cold as ice. If you're able to do more complicated work, and people like you or somebody gives you a chance to do it, all of that comes into play. If they don't like you and you could do it, you won't get a chance. You aren't going to be able to do it, because they don't like you.

On the Job training (OJT) is, above all, an opportunity to showcase one's ability to do the work. One African American journeyman reported that, as a young apprentice, he knew how to read blueprints, a skill he would not have been expected to know. He showed his skill by carrying blueprints onto the worksite and marking the prints with a highlighter so that someone standing at a distance could see that he had made sense of them. When an expensive mistake had been made, he was able to show the foreman the marked-up prints to reveal that he had foreseen that mistake and had already accounted for it. This same journeyman said:

I was only there to get knowledge. I wasn't there to be liked. I just wanted to know what they knew. [When one journeyman wouldn't explain how he did something] I kept asking like a kid in the store, "When are you gonna tell me?" I was there to work this guy to learn as much as I can, not let him grind you down, make him teach me anything he can, so I can get my game up and then I can go onto the next job.

Another African-American journeyman reported that as an apprentice, he "really had to fight to get into the spotlight," to attract the attention of journeymen who would then teach him the craft. Thirty years after his apprenticeship, he reported:

> There are people today that did not do well, who still are not very good journeymen, because they didn't get that help. They struggled through, and they still struggle today because they didn't get that help.

The community of practice as an economic unit

In order to understand how learning happens in a unionized apprenticeship program we have to expand the unit of analysis beyond the interaction between apprentice and journeyman and move to a large scale where we can see other players in the industry. This means the contractors, the unions, and public agencies, as well as the apprenticeship programs, just to name the obvious ones. All these players relate to each other in ways that are defined by contracts. The logic of the relationships is fundamentally economic and is driven by the bottom line.

Like other workers, construction workers, no matter how much they love their jobs, are working primarily to make a living. They care very much about getting paid. "Follow the money" is a good guide. When a journeyman takes on an apprentice and spends more than the minimum effort to teach him or her how to do something, that journeyman is not just being generous. He is taking care of his own retirement benefits. Unionized construction benefit plans have to be funded by working union members who pay into those plans. Those working union members are the next generation.

The senior journeyman, in other words, and the retired journeyman who is drawing his pension, look to the upcoming apprentice to acquire the kind of skills that will make his labor sell for the maximum price on the labor market. This means that old and young are bound together in a *community of practice* which is shaped by the economics of the industry.

When an apprenticeship program accepts a new apprentice, it begins an investment in that apprentice that will eventually cost the union upwards of $50,000, according to one apprenticeship director. The apprentice is expected to repay many times through productive work over a lifetime. This means that union apprenticeship programs place high value on retention, high completion rates and longevity. In order to pay back the investment in training, the apprentice needs to survive and work a full twenty or thirty years. This raises issues of health and safety. One of our interviewees said:

> They want you to stay healthy so you can work a long time. When I worked non-union they didn't give a crap about you. Your body would be dead at the end of the day.

The non-union apprenticeship programs, run by the Associated Builders and Contractors (ABC), are not structured around an economic unit that links the generations of workers to each other. Instead, they operate like school-based learning, where individual competition and grades serve a gate-keeping function that is as important as learning itself.

The economic unity of the *community of practice* in the unionized building trades is mostly invisible to the ordinary observer. Seeing workers moving deliberately from one task to another as you walk past a construction site, it's hard to see how the money flows. Without those connections, however, journeymen would not have a stake in the training of apprentices. Signatory employers, who have to hire union workers, would not allow the presence of apprentices on a building site unless they were confident that this was the only way for them to be trained. Apprentices would not be able to get a foot on the bottom rung of the ladder unless their training would serve as an investment that would pay off for the older workers someday.

The Building Bridges graduates who did not get a foot on the bottom rung of the community of practice of a unionized trade were outside this set of economic agreements. There was no one who had an economic stake in their success. No one else would benefit from the hours spent pounding the pavement or trying to scrape up the $500 application fee.

The concept of a *community of practice* works well for studying the way learning is passed along in any organization that hopes to survive for more than one generation of leadership. If an organization decides that it needs to pass along its memory, traditions and power to a new generation, there are things that it should do and things that it should not do. It is also easy to predict an organization's survival into the future by noticing how newcomers, or outsiders who want to get on the first rung of the ladder, are treated.

CHAPTER 10:
GARMENT SHOPS: PROBLEMS AND SOLUTIONS

> Employers forget that employees are human. The
> employer says, "Give me what I want. Sew what I want
> you to sew, do what I need you to do. I don't want to
> listen to your problem."
> When the member tells me a problem, she wants me to
> get more money in her pocket.
> — Doll Wilson, UNITE Business Agent

While Lave and Wenger's idea of *community of practice*
assumes that knowledge is a part of the culture of a
community, and that the community shares it and then
passes it along to the apprentice, they do not talk about
how the community creates the knowledge in the first place.
Boreham and his colleagues do. Boreham says that *Work
Process Knowledge* is the product of problem-solving. People
create new knowledge when they solve problems. When
people get together for the purpose of solving a problem,
they will draw something from everyone. Many voices
will contribute. The result will be new knowledge that has
a theoretical dimension. That is, it generalizes beyond the
immediate problem at hand. Then the new theory is tested,
an application of *Kolb's Learning Cycle.*

This chapter puts another twist on learning at work. It
illustrates how representation works to create, systematize
and preserve knowledge that is created through *Work Process
Knowledge* theory. The word "representation" here means
the process by which the concerns of one or several people
are adopted by someone else for the purpose of addressing
them. Broadly speaking, representation can be informal, in
the sense of one person listening to another person and then
carrying what the person said to another level, or it can be
formal representation, as in a labor union, where shop chairs

or business agents have the explicit job of representing other workers. Problems, issues, concerns among workers get carried up through the representation system and dealt with, if possible, through some aspect of the bargaining process. At each step this is also a process of learning.

In this chapter I will talk about formal representation as it has evolved in an old, established workplace in the garment industry. In this case, the accumulated knowledge created by problem-solving has persisted across multiple generations. But it is still being re-created as new problems in the social relations of work arise. I want to show how much – possibly all – the knowledge of how to do the work and run the business has become incorporated into the practice of representation even as the industry itself dies.

Representation creates knowledge

Representation is not just people communicating with each other all on one level, the way people communicate on a team. Representation is a staircase of communication. It begins at the bottom, with a person who has a problem. The problem is talked about and debated. If there is a union, everyone knows or should know what the next step is. "You need to call the union about this," someone will say. The person on the other end of that call is supposed to know what kinds of questions to ask and how to evoke a useful version of what happened. Then the problem gets passed up through steps that are defined in the contract until it ultimately gets addressed by those with the power to solve it. If there is no union and no authorized staircase of representation, the problem may or may not be passed up to someone who knows what to do next. If there is no one at the top of the communication staircase who has the power or will to do something about it, the problem may become standard operating procedure.

Problems start as production problems—a machine that

doesn't work right, a distribution of materials that is unfair, a demand to produce that can't be met—but the staircase of representation treats them as human relations problems and they are ultimately resolved, or not, by adjusting those relations. The mechanic comes or doesn't come; the distribution is changed or not, the demand is reduced or not. But without this problem-solving communications structure, and without representatives who have the authority to bring the problem to a solution, the solution to the problem would not exist. Over time, as this new knowledge accumulates, it becomes a broad overview of the workplace and possibly the whole industry, seen from the point of view of the workers.

As problems are solved, the workers who were involved in the process hold onto the lessons they have learned. They also share this knowledge with others in other sections of the shop. Over a longer period of time, this learning is shared with workers in other work sites and becomes broadly known throughout the industry. The process of representing workers creates more and more knowledge, while at worksites without representation, this kind of knowledge is not accumulated and is not retained to the same degree.

At the time that I worked for UNITE, the Union of Needletrades and Industrial Textile Employees, before its merger into UNITE HERE (Hotel Employees and Restaurant Employees), the union represented twenty or thirty garment shops employing over a thousand workers in Philadelphia. A generation ago there had been thirty thousand workers in the Philadelphia locals of the union. Some of the workers in these shops were second or third generation in the same shop. Mothers, sons and daughters worked together.

They made gorgeous things: tuxedos, alligator bags, wedding dresses, beautiful suits, fine shirts, military uniforms, drum major costumes. They made the kinds of full-length cashmere winter coats that cost as much as a car. Sometimes you can find their garments today in high-end thrift shops, selling to a third or fourth owner. Needless to say, the men and women who worked for this union dressed magnificently, often in clothes they sewed at home after work. However, their pay had been going down for a generation, and all the shops were under threat of closure. Before about 1970, when globalization started to sweep the garment industry into Mexico and eventually Asia, people were making $14 to $17 an hour under piece rate, where they are paid for each operation they finish. Thirty years later, many were making less than $10 an hour and working less than forty hours a week.

Problems in social relationships are always new

After generations of collective bargaining and union contracts, you might think that very little "new knowledge" could be created out of problems that arose in these shops. Social relationships involving human beings, however, are always changing. Just as they did nearly a hundred years ago, problems begin at the bottom. They are shared, debated, passed upward, negotiated, solved, and often incorporated into the written documents that govern the relationships of that workplace. Over time, they form a body of knowledge that seems to encompass everything possible. However, there is always some new problem generated by the sheer fact that the two concurrent *activity systems*, workers trying to make a living and owners and employers trying to run the business and make a profit, have to be constantly re-aligned.

Whereas grievance procedures in some union contracts run to pages and pages, the first step in the process for settling problems in this industry was stunningly simple, and probably word-for-word what it had been when it was first bargained. The shop chair simply gets up and walks over to the supervisor and tries to get the problem fixed. The American Clothing and Textile Workers Union (ACTWU, one of the predecessors of UNITE before various mergers) contract states:

> All grievances and disputes arising in the shops shall be adjusted if possible between the shop chairman and the foreman or other person in charge of plant. Such grievances shall be adjusted, whenever possible, after working hours.(ACTWU contract 1994)

I never saw anyone wait until after working hours.

However, the range of problems that the "adjustment" process is meant to fix is vast. When I worked for this union, workers were frustrated with how little money they were making. They felt they had a right to a fair workplace despite the ever-worsening conditions of the industry. They were certain that the employer was always trying to see what he could get away with. They knew the difference between being on piece rate and being on time rate, where you get paid by the hour. They understood piece rate as a management system involving punishments as well as rewards. They were watchful about the loss of earnings that are the result of disruptions in the work flow. They also cared about their product and worried about the effect of the piece rate incentive on quality. The union representative had to receive all these and other worries, talk to the workers, re-frame the problem and carry it to management and then back, often doing the whole thing in front of a gathering of agitated workers.

Often, the union representative took on responsibility for actually teaching workers how to do their jobs better. The representative had to function in a workplace with a fragmented, often linguistically segregated workforce, in the midst of competition among workers, and under the threat of the employer and even the union leadership to let the shop close and eliminate jobs. Nor could the union representative count on a collective response to problems at the shop or union level. He or she was also aware of the enduring consequences of a failure to resolve problems.

Historically, the announcement that there was a problem was made by the workers simply stopping work. Workers slowed their machines, the shop went quiet, and the supervisor would pop out of his office in a panic. One shop chair, now retired, remembered when he reversed a management rate-cutting decision by leading workers into the men's room where they all pretended, loudly, to have bowel cramps for several hours.

How piece rate links production to earning

If we go back to *Activity Theory* and think of this workplace as having two activity systems running together—the workers' activity of earning a living and the owner's activity of producing profit by producing garments—we can see that under piece rate, problems in one system will instantly create problems in the other system. Piece rate links the two systems together very tightly. Where work is measured in threads and stitches, earning a living is measured in pennies. A worker who has a faulty machine or who gets only difficult pieces to sew will slow down production. When one worker's production slows, so does that of the next person and the next. This immediately becomes a human relations problem for the union.

To illustrate the complexity of these rates, here is part of a piece rate sheet from a shop that made children's fancy clothes and is now closed. The whole rate sheet is eighteen pages long in its entirety. Even so, it only covers assembly: putting together elements of an outfit like shirt, belt, pants and necktie, hanging them on a hanger, etc., but not sewing. This document would be kept in a plastic folder where it could be referred to quickly to by a floor supervisor. The original, which I was allowed to photocopy, was yellow and wrinkled with use and had been marked up over the years with penciled changes.

First, there is a basic rate, in this case, for "a child's fancy outfit." These are the kinds of combination outfits that you might give as a holiday present: little pants, suspenders, a shirt with a tie and pocket handkerchief with a bunny rabbit on it, all on a hanger and wrapped in plastic.

Then there are add-on values for special features. The values displayed below are "add on" values. "SAM/Dozen" means Standard Allotted Minutes per dozen outfits. Note that for the add-on values, we are talking about fractions of minutes that are carried out, in one place, to five decimal places.

I chose to copy this part of the piece rate sheet because it showed the work of one particular woman, in this case, a forty-year-old African-American woman who was tall and slender and wore her hair in a tight bun. She would put her headphones on the moment she started working. "I put on my music and run," she told me. Picture her operating a sewing machine, one of about twenty such operators, in the middle of an open loft in an old brick factory building. Maybe there is heat or air conditioning; maybe there was a 5-gallon water cooler and paper cups. Some shops had no heat; most had no air conditioning. At one end of the loft, bolts of fabric stand waiting to be spread and cut; at the other end, the little outfits are packed into boxes for shipping.

Item

Shirts & blouses/sweaters...SAM/Dozen
attach double jet clip with string on both ends of shirt...2.28
stuff tissue in body ...4.1724
stuff tissue in sleeve long...2.600

stuff tissue in sleeve short...2.400
hang tag to button....850
straight pin collar...1.675
bowtie on collar...1.550
remove sobar stickers... .375
button shirt/button/doz.....4514
tie neck on collar...2.200
size sticker to hanger....98496
safety pin bowtie, ribbon or decorative item...2.750
safety pin beret, jeff cap, or visor w/2 safety pins...3.543
sailor sash under sailor collar and tie...5.690
jet clip long sleeves together...1.788
turn cuffs up on sleeps or bottom of pant leg...1.940
extra brush on fleece items... .150

As you can see from the short selection of the piece rate sheet, calculating what one should expect to be paid for one's work is no simple matter.

The base calculation would start with a SAM of 23.48 minutes for a dozen assembled items. If the job required that tissue be stuffed in a short sleeve, then the value 2.400 would be added on; if the item was fleece and needed an extra brush, the value of .150 would be added on. This total (25.63 SAM/ doz.) is then multiplied by the base hourly pay rate (which was $6.50 per hour at that time) divided by 60 (to get the pay rate per minute) to get .1083333. The final "price" of the operation, which is the total assembly of a dozen items at 25.63 standard allotted minutes per dozen, is 25.63 times .108333, or $2.78. In order to "make rate," or earn $6.50 per hour, she would have to produce 2.3 dozen or 28 items every hour. Minimum wage at that time was $5.15. She usually produced more.

Did she actually calculate these fractions of minutes as she sewed, adding up what she was earning, all the while listening to her music through her headphones? Probably not, although people learn to calculate all kinds of numbers if their ability to pay the rent depends on it. Jean Lave showed this in her work on everyday math in the grocery store; Sylvia Scribner showed how dairy delivery workers calculated how to pack a create with bottles and jars of many different volumes (Scribner, 1997). This woman could certainly figure out how her speed of work set her pay, when she was being cheated, or when a disruption in the flow of work made her less than optimally efficient. These were typical problems that she and other piece rate workers would bring to the attention of shop chairs and union reps.

How workers feel about piece rate and "fairness"

Basically, these workers know how piece rate works and they hate it. They spoke enviously of people who were on time rate:

> When you're on time rate -- You're going to get that wage no matter what. You're going to make that $10 an hour. You're not having to fight for every penny and watch everything you do. Every time you go to the bathroom. Every time you blow your nose.

But while they felt piece rate was fundamentally unfair, they also believed that somewhere, somehow, it should be possible to finally define "fair" and have a fair deal under piece rate:

> If you bust your hump to make ten dollars an hour, and you do your job correctly, you should have the ten dollars an hour.

They should not adjust. They say, I really want

you to trim this thread, or I want you to check this out, or measure this out, they'll add something to your job in order to change the rate so that you're not going to make as much money. That's not fair.

The sense that a fair deal was possible even today may have been a belief left over from another time. But union representatives could still use that belief in fairness to push through a solution to a problem. A union rep told me:

> There were two ladies that were hemmers. One was named Red, she was a good worker, she made $7.50 to $8.00 an hour. Then there was Sally who was a little slower but brings in the minimum. She makes $6.75 to $7.50. When they have good work, easy work, they use Sally. They only put Red on it when they need the two operators. So Red would get the hard work that slowed her down. She complained to me. So I went to the supervisor, I said this is not fair, the work is not being distributed on an equal basis. Red is not being treated fair and Sally is not being treated fair either. Give her some help and see if she can pull herself up. So she did. Now both of them get good work and bad work.

Sometimes a serious problem could actually get fixed by appealing to fairness. The rep told this story:

> I have this one lady who is seventy-one years old. She's sassy. She has only 10 years in and she can't retire. I didn't know she was that old. She doesn't want anyone to know she's that old. So just last week they were giving her a hard time. They said, "You're not a rate-maker." Now this lady has

made rate. We got together. Me, the shop chair, this lady, and the supervisor. I said, "Do you think she doesn't have feelings? The supervisor said, "I didn't mean to insult her." This lady said, "I'm sick and tired of being harassed." The supervisor said, "I'm sick and tired of hearing from her," and walked out.

So we wrote up a grievance and I took it to the big boss, the plant manager. I picked up this lady in my car and took her with me. This lady said, "Let me do my job and leave me alone." The big boss said, "I will make sure the supervisor doesn't bother you. " I said, "Please give it to me in writing." So he wrote it down. He wrote, "I did not realize this was causing stress on you. We will do our best in the future." It took a spunky, sassy worker to do this.

This worker now had a piece of paper with writing on it that gave her protection from the harassment of the supervisor. But the same rep, speaking out of hearing of her members, said bitterly:

Fair is whatever you can get.

Dealing with competition among workers

"Fairness" is fragile. Sometimes workers start early, work through their break, or work into lunch. This is unfair to other workers. The union rep also has to manage competition among workers.

Say there's two people on waistbands. They'll watch, and they will accuse the bundle boy of not liking a certain person and giving one person all the big bundles, or all the same color so that she won't have to change thread, and the other will get all what we call junk work. And they lose money.

She may have to check the books and negotiate an arrangement that the workers will accept as fair:

> Marge was getting up and going to the bench and separating the work and bringing some to this woman Katy, and Katy was saying Marge was giving her all the junk work and taking the good work herself. So we went in the office and looked at the books. It turned out that Kate wasn't getting the junk work. You can tell by the tickets. But I agree, Marge shouldn't be giving her work. If anybody should be giving her work, it should be the supervisor or Ronnie the bundle boy.

Workers cut corners, affecting quality, in order to squeeze out minutes of production time. The union rep has to deal with this, too:

> You're in such a hurry to make money that you don't do certain things you're supposed to do. You are supposed to random check your pants, when you finish five pair. If something's wrong with your machine you call the mechanic. You're supposed to clean your sewing machine, you're supposed to oil your sewing machines. The examiners who have the automatic trimmers, the threads all go into this hose and into this tube -- every day they're supposed to take it off and empty it. They're supposed to oil those machines, they're supposed to clean them. But they don't because they don't want to take time away from money.

Dealing with employer strategies for using the lowest-paid workers

Fairness, as a tool for the union rep to use in arguing for a solution to a problem, has its opposite in management rights. Based on the concept of management rights, which appears in every contract, the employer has the power to change the price of an operation. A shop chair described how she knew that the employers do intentionally, regularly, change job values:

> Different times that I've been in the office -- with like Alice, who makes the prices, and then Gino, and the boss, they're talking about different prices. They say, This is what it costs us to make a pair of pants. Now, if we give little bit more to this person, if we add a little bit of money onto their price, it's going to cost us more to make each pair of pants.

When someone is "making out," or making too much money, that person's job will be retimed or the rate will simply be cut:

> From what I've seen in every clothing shop that I've worked at, as soon as they see you making a little bit more than what they think, they will find a way to cut you back. They will find a way.

> Lewis' mother, when she was examining, she was going like crazy.

> When they checked back on the records they saw she was making a heck of a lot. So they cut

the rates for all the examiners. She's the one that spoiled it for all those examiners because she was taking home the money.

Switching people from one job to another to make the maximum use of the lowest-cost workers happens frequently. A union rep had to step in and fix this:

> This lady was listed as substandard which meant she was making $5.05 an hour or minimum wage at that time. She complained, and they gave her 8 weeks, and she made rate but they were still shopping her around as if she hadn't. I complained to the district manager. I said, this lady has made rate. She filed a grievance. It took me 6 months to get it fixed, but they paid her $1 for every hour she'd worked substandard. They owed her an apology, too, but she didn't get it.

The freedom of the employer to manage the work, to shift workers from one task to another, to classify workers according to their productivity, and to change operations and even to change the rates for operations, means that the shop chairs and union representatives are continuously engaged in discovering, verifying, and then trying to rectify changes that either violate the contract or custom and practice directly, or are merely unfair. This is the creation of the *Work Process Knowledge* of the human relations of piece rate.

Dealing with disruptions in the flow of work

Disruptions in the flow of work do not necessarily cost the employer anything. If the work is completed by the delivery date, when it is done prior to that is of little concern. But disruptions in the flow of work cost the workers more than just the money they might have made that hour or day. Then the union rep has to step in.

The flow of work can be disrupted because it is being distributed unfairly, or because the quality of the work has been affected, or because there is simply not enough work coming through the shop or because there is a breakdown. Work is distributed in bundles. Usually each bundle contains the makings of a dozen items. But some bundles, for example of unusual sizes or salesman's samples, may have only the makings of one or two items. When a worker gets one of these bundles, it slows her down:

> That's why I think about piece rate work, you can make out if you've got the work to do it with. But you can get stuck with bad work. This one girl was complaining. She had all these bundles with one, one, one, one. If you have a bundle with just one pair -- say, ten bundles with just one pair, you're opening and closing the strings all the time, ten times, which is very time consuming. You also have to write down your bundle number, how many pants were in the bundle, your lot number -- all that takes time, and the more bundles you have the longer it takes.

The shop chair here spoke to the girl who was complaining, and told her, "Just do it."

Sometimes neither the rep nor the shop chair can do anything:

> Frieda (the supervisor) kept giving me a helper when I didn't need a helper. Do you remember that? Well, I didn't need a helper. Joe (the BA) told Frieda, Kathy does not need this girl on this

job. She doesn't need a helper on this job, she can handle it herself. Frieda said Kathy's busy doing two jobs, this is one of her jobs. She needs this girl.

So the shop chair continued to have a helper, which meant that the helper did some of her work. The two of them, on one job, would regularly run out of work. When they had no work to do, they earned no money. The shop chair would have to call for more work in order to have enough production to make her "rate":

> So I'd be literally screaming up the steps to the bundle boy to bring me work. He'd bring me a bundle at a time. Sometimes the girl would go upstairs on her own herself and bring work back down. They'd bring me work that wasn't really ready for downstairs and let us press the seams open and they'd take it back upstairs. It was ridiculous.

Dealing with teaching as part of representation

Part of the work of the business agents in these shops was actually teaching. One rep described how she would talk to a worker who was having a problem. Note that the rep's definition of "problem" is that the worker is not making much money.

> If I pick up on someone who may have a problem, I come up and say, "You are doing the same job as so -and-so, why are you making less money?" Most of the time distribution of work is the typical problem, but it may be there is something they can do better. Maybe the floor lady can work with them.

When an operator sits down to sew, their emotions are 50% of what they can do. Then there's the cloth. If it's been cut with a hot knife, that can melt pieces of the garment together and it will take her longer to pull them apart and pick one up. Sometimes it's been cut a little bit on the bias, and it goes haywire. Then there's your knowledge of the machine. You and your machine have to be a team. It's like a car. You know when to shift gears in your car, when to put on the brakes, how long it takes to stop. Or maybe here comes a different style. It could be a month before the workers really know how to do it and are satisfied that the job is priced right.

You can find ladies who are 120% operators. Their depth perception is 100%. They can reach down beside them and separate the garment and lap it together and make the ends match without looking. That will give them a few seconds. Some of them can thread a needle with the machine going.

Dealing with the time-study

A critical point at which the business agent has access to the decision about how much money workers can earn is the moment when the price of piece rate work is set. Rates for a specific piece of work – for example, a new cut or style of garment - are set by having an "engineer," a management specialist trained in time-study, come and time a worker doing the operation. The engineer then writes up the time-study. This will set the rate for other workers who will be doing the same work later. The business agent talks to the worker and coaches her about what's going to happen.

Usually a piece rate is set when I'm not there. I try to tell the operator in advance what to expect, to allow her to look for things. I tell her don't let them intimidate you, speak out.

If an engineer is not secure, he'll put fast girls on a job and time them, and then set the rate a little above what they can do. If the boss uses them to set the rate – lets them prove that they can make 33 1/3 above 100% -- then they can never change it.

The danger is that a "fast girl" will be pressured into working even faster, and then that rate becomes the rate that other workers have to achieve.

After the rate is set and other workers have to try to work under it, there may be problems. It is now a collective problem, so the workers call the business agent, who investigates.

If the workers have a problem with the rate I go and look at the write-up. I look to see when the timing begins. Does the worker have to go get her work, or does the supervisor bring it to her? In real life, people have to leave their machines and go get work. Another problem is when the girls have to write down their tags. That takes time. Did they charge her for that time? Then there's PF&D -- personal, fatigue and down time. You'll find a different PF&D in every shop. It's in tenths of a minute -- 12 is average, 8 is when it's the same type of garment over and over. What PF& D did they use, and is it right?

The rate translates instantly into money. The complexity of the elements of the time study may obscure this, but everyone knows that even a slightly higher rate means fewer pieces earn the same amount or more money, and no one is confused about that. But negotiating to dispute the rates set by an engineer is difficult.

> Sometimes I can't do anything. I can't get the boss to give them any more money. It nags me. Down the road, it nags me.

The Business Agent mediates between two Activity Systems

One business agent, who had been assigned to organizing new shops for five years after working in a shop herself, put the two activity systems of her workplace in very clear words. Her skill lay in mediating between them:

> When the member tells me a problem, she wants me to get more money in her pocket. You have to know what you can get the employer to do. You have to learn what to say to the employer to get them to do what you want.

"Learning what to say" doesn't mean necessarily taking the employer's point of view:

> We can like each other as individuals but we don't deal with people the same way. Employers forget that employees are human. The employer says, "Give me what I want. Sew what I want you to sew, do what I need you to do. I don't want to listen to your problem." He only thinks about what he can get off her. If he listened to her tell him what the problem is, he could get more work out of her.

173

The basic conflict is never unclear: the worker sews to "get money in her pocket" and the employer "thinks about what he can get off her."

The lace mill

One of my last and most poignant experiences among the garment workers was a visit to a lace mill out in a rural area. Lace curtains still hang in thousands of windows in Irish and Italian neighborhoods in South Philadelphia. This mill would have been one of the places those lace curtains came from. It was so old that it once had been driven by a water wheel; it hung out over a little stream and was surrounded by old willow trees. The first room was as tall and long as a church, with high windows from the days before electric lights.

As we walked in, the union representative I was with suddenly darted off to one side down an aisle, grabbed a huge lever, and pulled it. Usually, the rule is that you never, never interfere with the machinery in a workplace that you are visiting. This woman had never been a lace-maker, either; she had been a sewing machine operator at a factory that made pajamas. But she had just stopped a loom because she noticed that a flaw was developing high up in the weave. The looms, which seemed to be made out of fat chunky pieces of cast iron and carved wood, stretched from the floor up 14 feet or higher into the rafters. How she saw the flaw emerging, I have no idea. She called out to a worker as we went on in, telling him what she had done. He said thank you and went to look at it.

Other than that one worker, the place seemed deserted. The owners were nowhere in sight. We went down some stairs into a room that seemed to be on the level of the millpond. In it were two elderly men and an old woman in work aprons.

The woman was assembling a gorgeous web of white threads spread out over a long table; one man was doing a drawing, and the other had a bench filled with bottles of glitter and paint and was experimenting with colors.

The funny thing was, the mill was actually closed. I have no idea whether anyone was getting paid. It was amazing that the lights were still on. The story was over; this was no longer a workplace. But they were still there, making lace. What activity system was in motion here?

CHAPTER 11:
AN OLD POWER PLANT: NON-STANDARD KNOWLEDGE

" We old timers know how to get ourselves out of trouble."
— Senior power plant operator

This chapter illustrates the importance of choosing the right unit of analysis. In this case, I was working on a project about safety at an old power plant and the choices were between two units of analysis, the "safety culture" of the plant and the actual physical condition of the plant. Activity theory was useful in both figuring out the difference between these two units of analysis and explaining why it mattered to my colleagues on the project.

People talk as if knowledge is always what is on the crest of the wave. The term "knowledge economy" means knowledge that is needed right now, that is marketable now and maybe tomorrow morning. Knowledge that was useful yesterday, like the cable splicing and installation that the man in Chapter 9 could do, is no good any more.

Using the word "consciousness" is a way to de-link knowledge from its connection with the cutting edge of the present. Consciousness is always in the present tense of the person who has it, no matter whether what is known is old or new. So is "readiness," in the sense that I have described it. But "knowledge" does not have to be cutting edge.

"Old" knowledge has a certain weight. The people who know it still carry it around. They don't forget it just because it's old. It occupies social space. It lives on in the people who possess it and even the people who know that someone else possesses it. It is like the landscape behind the drama of history. If you see a picture of a soldier with a horse or a farmer with an ox, you might think about the whole world of knowledge that it took to fight or work that way. The same goes for typesetters. How about automobile mechanics who were "grease monkeys" and lost their jobs when car engines became computerized? This would describe the man in Chapter 2 who unwittingly signed his own resignation papers. What happens to this knowledge? Does it disappear? Even when the places to use it are gone, it is still broad, emotionally charged, created and held collectively, and slanted in favor of its owner, like the other examples of knowledge described in this book. If it becomes forgotten, it leaves a significant void in an individual's sense of self. It is also a loss to the collectivity of workers who created it and formerly had access to it.

Furthermore, if a workplace is old, then "old" knowledge may be the right knowledge for that workplace.

In *Lies Across America: What Our Historic Sites Get Wrong*, James Loewen explains the domain of the sociology of knowledge.

> The sociology of knowledge studies what and how people think. By "knowledge," sociologists mean not only fact but also error, lies as well as truth, and also poetry, religion, law and other intellectual products that can hardly be labeled true or false. One approach the sociology of knowledge takes is to examine the institutional framework with which "knowledge" is produced. (Loewen 1999, p. 35).

Loewen is writing about what he calls sarcastically "the happy history on the landscape," promulgated by historic markers, monuments where some events took place, the absence of markers in other sites and the bulldozing and burial of still others. This is a very good book for people interested in labor history to read, because it is about the fights that have gone on over what gets memorialized and what doesn't. It explains why important labor history sites are unmarked or erased.

Loewen mentions error, "wrong knowledge," but this chapter is not about wrong knowledge. It is about "old" correct knowledge that would no longer be needed if equipment and machinery were repaired, updated and replaced. As much of the infrastructure (bridges, highways, buildings, power plants, dams) in the US has aged, there is a lot of this "old" knowledge out there, being used every day, saving lives and keeping the country going. Over the years, as each of these workplaces has deteriorated and become unique in its own way, the knowledge needed to operate it has also become unique.

Where "old" knowledge is used all the time

The institutional framework for this particular case of "old knowledge" is a small coal-fired power plant in the Midwest. The plant was built in 1941 and is still running. Years and years of deferred maintenance, ad-hoc repairs and temporary fixes have produced a workplace that is unique and that bears only a superficial resemblance to what it was when new. Yet it runs, operated by workers who know how to run it in its present state. Many of them have been there for twenty years or more, most of their working lives.

Their old knowledge is what they use to work safely and "go home at the end of my shift the way I came in" – a euphemism for not getting killed at work.

This example is a good one to use for exploring *Work Process Knowledge*, since that is what the "old knowledge" in this power plant consists of. This is a place where the workforce has had to solve problem after problem and has developed a way of running the plant that works but does not conform to standard operating procedures (SOPs) because the plant itself is not standard any more.

This case study is also a good example of the usefulness of *Activity Theory*. Activity Theory tells us to look first at the purpose of what's going on, in case we need to separate out the two different activity systems according to their purpose. These two activity systems are present in all workplaces. One is that people are doing work in order to earn a living. The other is that they are making the power plant generate electrical power from coal. In order to accomplish the first purpose, they have to survive the second. Because this is an example from real life, the two systems overlap and intersect in a messy way. However, distinguishing between them turned out to be key to getting some necessary repairs under way. In this case study, referring to *Activity Theory* made it possible for us to see what was the matter with the way management proposed to deal with the situation. We then made a counter proposal that worked.

A coal-fired power plant over 70 years old

There are many sites in the US where lack of investment in infrastructure has led to deterioration of equipment and machinery. Experienced employees have learned through trial and error how to coax production out of aging and faltering equipment and how to operate in a "safety zone." Whether or not the knowledge required to do this looks anything what it looked like fifty or seventy years ago, it is still knowledge. This is true in manufacturing, public infrastructure such as bridges, highways, electrical grids and dams, and in utilities such as power plants.

In spite of being non-standard and often requiring some creative and risky behavior, this is the knowledge that has kept these workers from having accidents and getting hurt. They have learned to live with their machines and keep them running and at the same time go home after their shifts with all their limbs intact. They are proud of it. This creates a problem for management both in terms of safety and in terms of training new hires. The choices for management are limited: train new hires in non-standard procedures; re-train senior employees in standard procedures but anticipate that modified equipment will not run in a standard way; or repair and replace equipment so that standard operating procedures can be followed. This last choice will require paying the substantial costs that disinvestment avoided. However, when a site deteriorates enough to become dangerous, the cost of accidents to workers, employers or the community gets set against the cost of repair.

In 2009 there were about 600 coal-fired plants in the US, most of them built between 1940 and 1970. They are a major source of air and water pollutants, the top 25 of them producing over half the sulfur dioxide emissions for the US. Workers at the particular plant I will write about supply steam heat to a major public entity and electricity to the grid from which other branches of the entity draw. Like any power plant, their workplace contains many potential hazards.

Our labor education program became involved at this plant when a new manager discovered that the workers were not wearing basic safety equipment like hard hats, safety glasses and gloves. These are standard equipment (PPE, or Personal Protective Equipment) in just about every workplace where there are moving parts. In a power plant, where heat, steam, high voltages, toxins, noise and moving parts surround the workers, these kinds of PPEs are like a uniform. However, when the manager ordered these workers to wear hard hats and other PPEs, they ignored him.

The manager said:

> I come in at night and it's…where's your hard hat?
> Or they see you and they grab it … and you know

what? There is probably a larger subset of guys now that do wear their hard hat all the time but there's still a very noticeable portion that do not.

The stalemate over the use of PPEs forced the manager to bring in some consultants. I was the labor educator on the consultant team with several human resources specialists and a systems analyst. The manager added:

> To be honest, I would be surprised if they didn't tell you they didn't feel it was necessary cause if they felt it was necessary they'd be wearing it. There's a reason they're not wearing it. Hopefully you guys can help us figure that out.

Why weren't they wearing PPE?

So what was the reason?

My first step, as the labor educator on the project, was to call over to the plant, which was unionized, and ask for the shop steward. Sure enough, I was put in touch with a man who had been working at the plant for many years. I went to see him and asked if he could explain why workers were unwilling to wear PPEs.

His response was to make a list of twelve longstanding serious hazards in the plant. These had all been discussed numerous times, either through a now-defunct safety committee (workers had stopped participating, out of frustration), through formal complaints that workers had made, or through ordinary workplace conversation. We wrote down everything on the list, in language I could understand. He then shared this list with the environmental officer, who was not a direct employee of the plant, but who had oversight of the plant as well as other associated operations. Together they added some details. The environmental officer signed off on this list as correct.

I took the list back to our team. At this point, although the project continued for many months, our actual analysis of the condition of the plant had gone as far as it would ever go. Nothing we learned about the condition of the plant from then on changed any detail. It should not surprise anyone that the shop steward had a complete and accurate list of all the serious hazards in the plant. This would be an example of *Work Process Knowledge*. What remained to be discovered by our team was what this had to do with the reluctance of some of the senior workers to wear PPE.

There was also a relatively new joint labor-management Safety Committee at the plant. Membership on the committee was mainly workers who volunteered because they had not given up on finding a way to get hazards fixed. This Safety Committee gave our investigating team a list of questions. The first two questions were:

> Why do plant personnel disregard safety directives?
> Why does management ignore safety concerns expressed by plant personnel?

These two questions summarize the stalemate. The "safety directives" which the plant personnel disregarded involved, primarily, wearing hard hats and other safety equipment such as respirators.

A pair of different questions from the same list indicated what the workers felt lay behind the stalemate:

> Does staff perceive that production trumps safety? Why?
> What budget concerns is management faced with? Does this impact safety?

Another way to express this stalemate would be:

Is this plant in fact a dangerous place to work?

Or.

Are the workers who refuse to wear hard hats simply being careless and insubordinate?

The research team then embarked on a long process of interviewing every regular employee at the plant, labor and management. The hope, agreed to in a meeting between the plant management and the research team, was that through the process of interviewing, followed by a report to the Safety Committee, a window of opportunity would open which would break the stalemate. Where this would lead we did not know.

At that point it was not within the scope of our team to officially evaluate the actual condition of the plant, although no one was arguing with the list of twelve hazards that the union had drawn up. While a "baseline audit" of the condition of the plant was part of the initial research design, it was cancelled.

Nor did the project plan call for an outside evaluation from either an industry safety council or from the State Department of Labor, which administers the federal Occupational Safety and Health Act for the public sector in that state. The hope was to resolve the stalemate "in house." Money was definitely a factor, but there was also a risk that too much investigation might find the plant in such bad shape that it would get shut down.

Therefore, lacking a directive to study the actual condition of the plant, the assignment became to "investigate the safety culture of the plant."

What does "safety culture" mean?

"Safety culture" is an approach to safety management that looks at attitudes and behaviors. It establishes a unit of analysis that does not include the physical plant, the actual machines or equipment that the workers have to work with. Therefore it excluded addressing whether the plant was actually dangerous or not. By choosing to investigate the "safety culture" it seemed that management had decided that "personnel disregarding safety directives" was the problem, not "safety concerns from plant personnel."

Within the safety culture literature, the term refers to attitudes, procedures, organizational capacity and behaviors such as employees' willingness to follow directives (Diaz-Cabrera, Herandez-Fernaud, Isla-Diaz 2007; Reason 1997; Human Engineering 2005). The concept was brought into use following the Chernobyl accident in 1986. Studies of the safety culture of various environments are often questionnaires that focus on trust, training, cooperation, attitudes toward management, communication and information-gathering. Safety culture, in these studies, refers to a set of social relations, not to the condition of the physical environment. There is clearly a normative aspect to these social relations: the purpose of the analytic tool "safety culture" is to support the creation of social relations in a workplace that will make that workplace safe. There are commercial programs to assess safety culture, which can be purchased by companies to do assessments of their own sites.

Safety cultures can be good or bad. According to R. Westrum (1996), every workplace has some kind of safety culture. There can be "pathological," "bureaucratic" or "generative" safety cultures. Westrum's typology of safety cultures is a matrix with six dimensions (adapted; five shown here). The type of safety culture that characterizes a particular environment can be found by comparing it to this matrix. Note that the verbs, with several exceptions, use the passive voice, dodging the question of, for example, "Is hidden by whom?"

Table 3. Comparison of Safety Culture Types (after Westrom, 1966)

Pathological	Bureaucratic	Generative
Information is hidden	Information may be ignored	Information is actively sought
Messengers are "shot"	Messengers are tolerated	Messengers are trained
Responsibilities are shirked	Responsibility is compartmentalized	Responsibilities are shared
Failure is covered up	Organization is just and merciful	Failure causes inquiry
New ideas are actively crushed	New ideas create problems	New ideas are welcomed

A safety culture can be changed by identifying practices such as hiding information or compartmentalizing responsibility, and then changing those practices. The desirable direction of change following Westrum's matrix is from left to right, from pathological (sick) to bureaucratic (rigid) to generative (effective). It also makes a difference whether information is hidden by or from management and whether failure is covered up by workers or management.

However, it should be obvious that nothing on this matrix ensures that management will address and fix the actual, dangerous conditions in the workplace. The Pathological Process will sweep the problems under the table and provide no solution. The Bureaucratic is unlikely to make any substantive improvements in the facility. The Generative holds out the possibility of fixing the problem, but it does not specifically demand it.

The focus on attitudes and behaviors begs the question

of what is going on in a plant that may be really dangerous and where a lot of the machinery doesn't work the way it is supposed to. The "safety culture" unit of analysis allows management to listen to the problems expressed by the workers without actually fixing them.

While I was working on this project, retired Steelworker Gary Gaines sent me a statement titled "Beware Behavioral Safety!" from Workers Uniting, the joint union of the Steelworkers and Unite, the largest labor organization in the UK. This statement warns that behavioral safety programs shift the focus of health and safety towards whether or not workers are using their PPE, and away from the actual condition of the plant. The Workers Uniting statement argues for "engineering solutions" that involve redesigning places in the physical plant where there are hazards, including ergonomic stressors and work organization problems such as understaffing or production pressures.

These two perspectives correspond to the two perspectives – conflicting – of the two *activity systems* in action at the power plant. While it was not surprising that the Steelworkers had figured this out, it was important for the research team to be able to begin our discussion of next steps by referring to a theory, *Activity Theory*, that had a track record of explaining many other situations.

Safety culture and the workers at the plant

When we asked workers directly about their understanding of the term "safety culture," many said that they had not heard it before. One third responded with answers that focused on equipment, not on attitudes:

Q: What does that term mean to you?
A. Doesn't mean a thing.
Q: What would it look like if there was one?
A: They would repair equipment and make sure

it was ready to come back instead of force feeding it and putting it back on before it is actually ready.

Twenty per cent specifically mentioned that the pressure to produce overrode the principle of working safely:

> It's a culture of safety as long as we're putting out steam and heat… They've got to keep producing because that's what we're here for.

> Let's produce, produce, produce. Oh, wait a minute – now we've got to do safety.

> It's money first, safety second.

The question about safety culture led workers to talk about knowledge. Referring to upcoming retirements of the most experienced workers, they said:

> Your knowledge base walking out the door; that's dangerous!

Here is a situation where we can show why a unit of analysis matters. As I explained in Chapter 5, "unit of analysis" means the smallest set of components of something that are necessary for its existence. Think of it as a molecule of a chemical compound or a cell in a biological organism. Compare the unit of analysis of "safety culture" with the unit of analysis of "making a living working at the power plant." The components which make up a 'safety culture" include communication, training, attitudes, behaviors, etc. You need to include all of these in your analysis in order to understand a safety culture. They do not, however, include anything physical. They do not include tools such as the acid bath, the scaffolding, the electrical system, the valves, the belts that carry coal to the boilers. Nor do they include the tools that the workers invent out of duct tape and mop handles or the out-of-date alarm system. In other words, the safety culture is the wrong unit of analysis. It is a bogus strategy devised to placate the workers' complaints by giving the appearance of addressing workplace problems but only serving to delay the actual remediation.

In *Activity theory*, the unit of analysis links the physical reality where something is happening to the people who are doing it and the reasons they are doing it. This is the "tools" part of the unit of analysis, at the top of the triangle model. It includes machinery, equipment, communication systems—everything you might use to do the job.

Mapping the workplace

We were able to integrate the workers' view of the physical condition of the plant during our interviews. We did this by giving them maps of the first floor of the plant and the basement. We then asked them to circle areas where they had safety concerns. By asking workers to mark where hazards existed, we were able to go past the "safety culture" approach. We were no longer just talking about how people behaved. We were talking about physically dangerous equipment. Forty-four different kinds of hazards were identified.

One power plant worker, circling a spot on the map, gave us this answer:

> We had a leak in our pre-scrubber. It was leaking all over the floor and the acidity level was one and two, very acidic. They tell the operators to put soda ash on it to neutralize. OK, so we do that for a while. Then they come out and they say, "Well, you guys should probably wear…" and they give us little rubber rain suits to wear while we're doing

this in case any of it drips on us. Then a week later or two weeks later they come out and say, "Well, you guys really should have these acid resistant suits on instead of the rain suit." Now this is after two weeks of shoveling this soda ash during this leak. The whole time, the leak is only the size of a nickel. Why not, instead of putting people in positions to where they could possibly be hurt, shut it down for a few days and get it repaired?

Another power plant worker marked a place on the map and said:

Inside the jet bubbling reactor there is an agitator with a shaft that goes all the way from the ceiling to the floor of this tank. You can't turn if off if there is material in the bottom of the tank. I have to go into that tank with that shaft turning to get it clean... I have to leave the shaft turning. At one point in time, they wouldn't let me in there without having safety harnesses and lanyards on. The problem with that is, you get a lanyard wrapped around that frickin' shaft, you're going for a ride and you're probably going to lose some parts in the process...

It looked as if it was impossible to make the plant produce electrical power without requiring workers to take risks that might send them home different from the way they came in. That is, on a stretcher or in a body bag.

By getting everyone to draw their concerns on a separate map, we were able to see a difference between the kinds of safety concerns that management had versus the concerns workers had. While the management interviewees mentioned major pieces of equipment that were dysfunctional or temporary, but had been in place for years and were unsafe, the workers tended to mention the kinds of hazards they would encounter regularly while walking back and forth in the plant, such as hoses lying on the floor, tangles of live electrical wires stuffed into pans with dead wires, broken latches, steam leaks choked with a mop head and duct tape. Sixty-three percent of workers listed hazards from leaks, including steam leaks, flue gas, fuel oil and acid leaks. Fifty-nine percent mentioned electrical hazards such as water:

> This morning we came in and they had shut one of the boilers down. It started dripping water. And we had some welding to do and we use electricity to weld. When you're standing in an inch of water, really it doesn't make you happy…

Something that workers mentioned numerous times was the switch gear:

> When there's a half to three-quarters of an inch of coal dust on top of the breakers it's just a matter of time before it's gonna catch fire. All it takes is a spark. All it takes is a path from that 13,800 volts to ground and that's when the breakers blow up. I made a specific point to ask the safety committee and people who run the plant, "Can we have two electricians and that's what their job is, to clean those breakers?" They said no, they're running out of people.

A lead electrician, who was supposed to supervise eight electricians, confirmed this:

> Seven years ago, instead of eight electricians, they sent me four. So I felt like I've been four people

short for seven years. That's 28 man-years I've been behind on.

Workers not only operated the plant in the face of a continuous stream of breakdowns and patch jobs, but they did so doggedly in a spirit of heroic, joking sacrifice. This can probably be sensed by the tone of voice in which they answered questions. They saw their work as essential to the city: keeping the lights on for the community. One employee said:

> There is no spot in the plant that I would not go into, that I would refuse to take care of, my duties because I'm not gonna go home tonight.

But recurring emergencies are wearing. Another explained:

> At 2 in the afternoon, if you're like, Well, I just finished saving the plant and there was an emergency and I'm exhausted …when that's over and you say, OK, now I can go back and do my mundane stuff, it's tough to get in the groove. You know another emergency is coming along within 24 hours…

Some of them volunteered that they sometimes took risks themselves, noting that they had to in order to do their "duty," that is get their job done. Three workers responded with these comments:

> The training officer…can tell you how things are supposed to run. But it don't always run that way, and to make it through the night without getting reprimanded or whatever, you do what you got to do to get it running.

You can get splashed with acid or caustic and run take a shower. If you have a quick ten-second job where you can just get the job done, or at least secure something and then go wash your hands off – you know how much it's gonna hurt you, which is not very much at all in ten seconds...

I've done it too. I got burns, I got hit. It's my own fault. You want to get something done and you get involved with it. Then you start pushing safety things that you probably shouldn't do but you're going, "I just want to get this done." You got steam blowing everywhere. You've got to stop it blowing. You can't really close the valve. You put something over it just so it won't blow everywhere...My first thought is not to put on my hard hat. My thought is, "I got to take care of this problem out here."

This is the worker who told me that what he puts over a valve that is blowing is a mop head, and then he wraps it with duct tape.

Nonetheless, despite the near misses and some actual explosions, no one could think of any major accidents:

You hear about people all over the country having accidents in these kinds of plants and we haven't had a fatality. We've had some broken bones and stitches, and bad backs and things like that, but no one's been crippled or dead. Gotta be something said about that.

On the other hand, one senior worker said, "Everyone here is on a race between retirement and disability." Also, during our interviews, we could see scars on their hands and arms.

So why is it working?

So, how did they learn to run this plant? If it is so non-standard, so run-down that there are no standard operating procedures, how did they learn to make it work – and make it work for years with no fatalities? How do we explain the knowledge that they obviously had created in order to get the job done and keep the plant running?

Formal training was more typical of the newer hires. When asked how they learned to do their job, these younger, newer workers would report having earned an AS degree at a community college or having received other formal training, sometimes specifically safety training at a previous job. Their attitudes toward safety were distinctly different from the attitudes of the more senior employees. One new hire who had been there one month said:

> At Toyota, if something was a safety hazard, you stopped everything right there and got all the people out of the way. Here it seems more like, "Well, it's still gotta be done, just be careful."

Many of the more senior employees reported on-the-job training at the plant, although many had military, especially Navy backgrounds. Some mentioned that at one time the Navy was the main source of trained boiler operators; now that ships no longer run on boilers, that source of trained operators has dried up.

But for all the senior employees, the main training was on the job at this plant. Employees with twenty years or more in the plant responded to the question about how they learned their job with:

I just asked them guys, "Hey, I need to learn this, I need to learn that."

You were thrown into the job and it was up to you to learn it if you were going to survive... it was trial and error.

I've lived through the disasters.

When I walked in the door I was like a kid in a sandbox. There's not day that goes by that I don't sit there, "Why is that thing doing that?"

Learning from other guys who were doing it made me who I am.

I train you. You train her. You train him.

Although the question we asked was simply, "How did you learn to do your job?" the answers tended to come back in terms of "How did you learn to survive your job?" An employee who had been at the plant eight years described his on-the-job training. It was in-person, one-on-one integration into a *Community of Practice* followed by problem-centered collective reflection (*Work Process Knowledge*) because of the condition of the plant:

> Basically it was the senior guys when I first started here would come out and tell you this is this, this is this, this is what you do. You kind of pick up on it as you go. You start walking through the plant tracing systems out and hopefully you get an idea of what is going on. You walk through with a flashlight and you just kind of trace it out and see where the valves are. There's a lot of reasons for

doing this, not just know the plant, but also know where the valves are in case you have a steam leak or a fuel leak… so if something bad did happen you could follow down the line and isolate it.

The theme that ran through all the descriptions of on-the-job training, whether one-on-one or self-guided, was safety. Soon it became apparent to us that learning to do the job was identical with learning how to survive the job. Another employee said:

> If you understand how this machinery runs it's a lot easier to troubleshoot it and keep it running because some of it is very old… I realize how to mitigate and what to stay away from, what to just try to control, what to run from and when to say, "We can't deal with this…"

A fourteen-year employee described what he does to learn the plant:

> I'll stand there when I'm not out there [on the floor of the plant] for any particular reason, I'll just wander out there and stand and just kind of look around and think while I'm looking, where am I at and what are the potential hazards? And those are the ones that you physically see.

When these employees have time and space to study the plant, they are focusing on how to discern the hazards and how to prepare for dealing with them. Their learning and therefore their actual *Work Process Knowledge* is about safety. What they are learning, disguised as how to run the plant, is how to run the plant safely. Then, when the disaster comes – and several said it was just a matter of time -- they are as ready as they can be.

Keep the plant in the corral

One morning we came into the plant after a near miss and interviewed the lead operator, a 23-year employee, who had been on duty during the night. His state of being in "cruise control" sounded like the "collapse of sense-making" as noted by Rogalski, Plat and Antolin-Glenn (Boreham, Fischer & Samurçay, p. 134-147). He described what it was like to deal with a disaster:

> My job is I have ultimate responsibility for everything and all the people and the equipment. There's too many things to focus on so you're in sort of cruise. You're in cruise control and you're just going along making these observations and people are calling in and saying, "I'm gonna do this and I'm gonna do that," and I'm saying, OK, OK. It's just sort of coming at you. The power plant is like a wild horse or something. You've got it in a corral but you can't ride it. You can just sort of keep it in the corral. But that's what my primary job is, to keep the plant in the corral doing its thing. This thing is not only one big mechanical animal but it's like a life form in here. Even the things you can't see, like the responsibilities and the knowledge base ... it's all part of this beast.

He worried about passing this knowledge on to the next generation of operators, workers who had current job titles of Auxiliary Operators and the Utility Operators. He named the knowledge that his generation had accumulated "the knowledge to get ourselves out of trouble." It was broad knowledge about the whole system. Its purpose, and the purpose that motivated its creation, was survival. This meant that the knowledge itself had a slant, or bias, in favor of survival. If you pictured this knowledge as a map it would be a map of how to run the plant and not get hurt.

He explained:

> We [the Operators] were the ones who were taught by the old-timers. The new Auxiliary Operators and the Utility Operators, they just got bits and pieces of things. They never got the full story, so those guys are like, "Well, I know if you push this button this is gonna happen." They know what the end result is but they don't know the in-between part. We, the old timers, know how to get ourselves out of trouble. It's the guys who are going to be taking our place that don't have the knowledge to get themselves out of trouble.

Incidentally, when we asked what the consequences of working unsafely were, no one mentioned discipline as a consequence. One interviewee said, "I go up and whisper in the person's ear that they need to be taking care of that." Most people said, "You get hurt or someone else gets hurt." The consequence of taking a risk was direct: people got hurt. However, this was a plant where despite glaring examples of hazards, no major accidents had happened.

What was done

As of now, the accident that will make front page news, cause the evacuation of the plant and much of the town and trigger an investigation by the Environmental Protection Agency and other agencies has not happened. But changes have occurred. I would argue that these changes can be attributed to the resistance of the senior employees to wearing hard hats, safety glasses, gloves and other basic Personal Protective Equipment (PPE) in defiance of management directives. You might even say that this refusal was a sort of non-violent protest against the condition of the plant.

Changes included:

- appointing a senior employee as the training officer;
- providing him with an office and a computer;
- convincing him to commit to postponing his retirement;
- developing a consensus and review process for recording the operating procedures actually used by workers;
- building a special portal on the plant website where updated procedures were posted in an accessible way;
- Management changed the crew structure so that workers bid to be on the crew of the lead operator from whom they might expect to get the most training (and therefore become capable of passing a promotion exam);
- The environmental and safety officer held "safety tailgates" in which lead operators met and discussed specific safety problems;
- The Safety Committee went through the plant with cans of yellow and red paint and marked objects to be moved into their proper place or else dumped.
- The whole workforce participated in workdays when literally tons of unused and unusable equipment were hauled away. Simply clearing the traffic lanes made an enormous difference in the plant.
- The plant management made a demand on upper management for funding for large scale repairs.

Using the terminology of *Activity theory*, it appears that focusing on the "tools" element of the activity system, the physical reality, had opened up a conflict within the activity system. The way this conflict shook the balance of power of the system was to strengthen the voice of the workers and push the argument for actually repairing the plant into upper management's awareness. By refusing to use standard PPE (tools), the workers violated some of the historical norms of workplace safety. In workplaces like this power plant, ordinary rules and customs would require wearing of PPE. The fact that senior employees who had the knowledge base to "get the plant out of trouble" were refusing to wear PPE got the attention of management which expected to run the plant in the generally accepted way. This conflict revealed the real balance of power in the plant. Management could not run the plant. Management could not even threaten or apply discipline. Given the unique knowledge of these senior workers, who knew better than anyone else how to run the plant (better than the manager, in fact), threatening or disciplining them would not have been effective. Something else had to be done. By refusing to obey a simple safety rule, the senior workers created a stalemate in the Safety Committee which started the dominoes falling.

At the time that we presented our first feedback to a group of the actual workforce, there was still skepticism about the possibility of improvements in the actual physical safety of the plant. This skepticism was expressed by a senior lead operator who, in the feedback meeting, said he planned to continue to wear short-sleeved shirts at work. Our report back also coincided with the retirement luncheon of another one of the senior employees. Workers said, "Another piece of the knowledge base walking out the door."

However, with the addition of our interviews and our report, the whole project created some leverage for plant management to push the problem up the ladder and negotiate with upper levels of the entity's financial structure. In a few weeks, the Director of Utilities informed the group that a report of the team's work was in the hands of the top officers and that the Director's full budget request had been granted, for the first time. "Of course, we could spend a hundred million dollars," he added, which was apparently more than he had been able to get.

CHAPTER 12.:
WHY STUDY THIS KNOWLEDGE?

> Every hill, every valley, creek, canyon, gulch, gulley, draw, point, cliff, bluff, beach, bend, good-sized boulder and tree of any character had its name, its place in the order of things. An order was perceived, of which the invaders were entirely ignorant.
> — Ursula K. Le Guin, *A Non-Euclidean View of California*

Why study this knowledge? The short answer is, "Because people made it." It is a product of human imagination, just like a garden, a bridge, a map or a book. It doesn't matter whether the industry where it is made is the cutting edge of what can get someone hired today. It exists. It is what is going on in the minds and within the communities of the people who possess it. It is knowledge about social relationships. It has substance, beauty, weight, depth and as we have seen, it saves lives and makes decent work possible.

There are two manifestations of this knowledge that may raise this question more sharply. One is obsolete or non-standard knowledge. This could be the knowledge of the union representatives in the garment shops or the knowledge of the power plant workers. The other is knowledge of how things ought to be – not how they actually are, but how they should be if they were done right, the way the worker who has to do it thinks it should be done.

What is the knowledge of the power plant workers worth when the plant gets upgraded and runs on standard operating procedures? What is the knowledge of the garment workers' union reps worth when the shops close?

By intentionally studying obsolete knowledge, we repudiate the idea that the only value of knowledge is what you can sell it for. This measure of knowledge is gaining force in the world of education, including and especially adult education and education for work: the value of a body of knowledge is what you can sell it for, that is, its price on the labor market. When we talk about "skills" training we are usually talking about employer-defined knowledge that is needed at a certain moment and at a certain price. By this standard, obsolete knowledge is worthless.

By studying obsolete knowledge, however, we confer value on what people have created in order to make a decent life. There is no standard of value that trumps that.

In a way, it's a lot like studying a language, a "dead" language like Latin or Greek, for example. There are also languages that have recently gone extinct, like those of the various California Native Americans, or have only a few living native speakers. Why try to explore the consciousness that is embodied in these languages? Without trying to answer this question directly, it may be enough to say that for some people, entering into a different way of being human through the portal of language is an adventure. And every body of knowledge has its own unique way of knitting together its part of a language.

The other kind of knowledge that has made an appearance in these case studies is knowledge of how things are supposed to be. People may hold this knowledge as a certainty despite the fact that it pictures a situation that doesn't really exist. It too is broad, shared, collectively created, slanted toward the perspective of workers, and infused with powerful emotion. It, too, is learned in ways that can be analyzed using the learning theories we have talked about. Take, for example, the knowledge of people who work in a bad situation but can imagine how it could be improved.

This is the particular burden of public sector workers like healthcare workers, park rangers, food safety inspectors, Environmental Protection Agency investigators and teachers in systems that have been defunded so that they no longer can actually do what they were created to do. Like obsolete knowledge, the knowledge of how things are supposed to be is real knowledge. It has just lost its footing, or rather its power, in the real world. The people who possess it, like the teachers in Chapter 2, carry out their day-to-day assignments while confronting simultaneously what is and what should be, and the differences between them.

A term from psychology for this is "cognitive dissonance." This refers to the tension experienced by a person who believes one thing and acts, or is required to act, contrary to that belief. Workers who perform work that they know is risky or harmful, or who are required to perform their work in a way that is not the best or the right way to do it, experience cognitive dissonance. If workers in this situation believe they are alone, they are among the loneliest people in the world. When these workers come forward and insist that their work is done right, the tension is reduced. "At least I don't feel as if I'm going crazy," one might say. The worker may get into more trouble this way, but at least the tension of cognitive dissonance will go away.

This introduces the next chapter, which is about two situations involving teachers.

CHAPTER 13:
TEACHERS: WHEN THE CITY IS THE CLASSROOM

> Have the voices of "stakeholders" — students, their
> parents and families, educators, and citizens who support
> public education — been strengthened or weakened? Has
> their involvement in public decision-making increased
> or decreased? ... According to these measures, the mega-
> foundations' involvement has undoubtedly undermined
> both democracy and civil society.
> — Joanne Barkan, *How Mega-Foundations Threatened Public
> Education*

In Chapter 2 we saw three teachers who were working, or
trying to work, under conditions that they knew were wrong.
They compared their situation with that of the stationary
engineers who were respected for what they knew, had the
power to control their work, and were paid well for it.

Recently, teachers in Chicago and San Francisco have
engaged in two struggles over control of their work. In
Chicago, the fight was initially over a contract for public school
teachers. In San Francisco, it was initially over accreditation
for the community college. Without accreditation, colleges
lose all federal, state or local funding and must effectively
close. Both struggles have been, overall and so far, successful.
In both cases, the teachers have brought what they know
about teaching to the way they organized their fight. They
let that guide them in building strength both in their union
and in their cities. They treated their members as if they were
a *community of practice* and their two cities as if they were
classrooms.

We can see the application of learning theory in their
strategies.

They both had to learn who their opponents were (*Activity
theory*). Their opponents were more than just the faces on the

other side of the bargaining table (in the case of Chicago) or the President of the accrediting commission (in the case of San Francisco). Their enemies could be identified by their purpose, which was opposed to the purpose of the teachers. They had to learn who was on their side and who was not.

They both had to invest in major fights that went through many stages. In the case of Chicago, the fight started in the 1980s. In the case of San Francisco, the union had only a short time – really, a few months - to recover the collective power that it had had in the 1980s and 1990's (*Kolb's Learning Cycle*). Both unions tested strategies and invented new ones.

Both opened their *community of practice* to their members and their cities.

Both solved problems by gathering people together in study groups, working groups, formal meetings and mass meetings (*Work Process Knowledge theory*). They publicized their solutions in press releases, websites, mass one-on-one conversations, picket lines, demonstrations and occupations.

Realizing that the struggle went beyond the immediate contract or accreditation fight, the teachers posed the question, "What is education for?" This was not a question about what they were doing in their individual classes. They were asking on behalf of public education generally. For whom, by whom, and for what purpose?

In order to appreciate the challenge the teachers were facing, we have to look back at the big shift in the purpose of public education over the last fifty years.

"A successful democracy premised on an educated citizenry"

The historic answer to "For whom, by whom and for what purpose?" is that education is for "a successful democracy premised upon an educated citizenry." This was what the

State of California's *Master Plan for Higher Education* declared in 1960. This plan became incorporated into the State Constitution. To achieve an educated citizenry, all higher education including the community colleges, state colleges and the universities, was supposed to be accessible to anyone who could "benefit from instruction" and tuition-free.

Free tuition? In a speech given in 1958 James L. Morrill, President of the University of Minnesota, reacted with outrage to a proposal to charge tuition:

> This notion [of paying for higher education by charging tuition and fees] is, of course, an incomprehensible repudiation of the whole philosophy of a successful democracy premised upon an educated citizenry. It negates the whole concept of wide-spread educational opportunity made possible by the state university idea. It conceives college training as a personal investment for profit instead of a social investment. No realistic and unrealizable counter-proposal for some vast new resource for scholarship aid and loans can compensate for a betrayal of the "American Dream" of equal opportunity… (*California Higher Education Master Plan*, p. 173)

This tuition-free system worked like this: the state colleges and universities could select a certain per cent of high school graduates, but the community colleges, according to the Education Code (Section 5706) would "accept any high school graduate and any other person over eighteen years of age…capable of profiting from the instruction offered." (*California Higher Education Master Plan*, p. 70).

"Capable of profiting" seems unthinkably broad today. But it was nothing new in 1960. The same language had been used in the 1947 report of the Truman Commission (titled *Higher*

Education for Democracy). The Truman Commission proposed the establishment of community colleges all over the country open to *anyone who could profit or benefit from instruction*. Since the developmentally disabled, professionals, the elderly, the non-English speaking and people who have advanced degrees can all profit from instruction, and since instruction can be in any field, including language, art appreciation, wellness, and citizenship, as well as vocational, liberal arts, humanities and sciences, this meant that community colleges were truly open-door public institutions for lifelong learning.

Within this system, it was possible for a student to enter a community college in need of basic skills and eventually climb the ladder into an advanced degree. The ladders were real. There was also plenty of room for people to move laterally. You didn't have to be locked into a credential or degree plan. You could try a music class or learn a new language. A student with limited English or math skills could sit next to a student with a PhD and both could profit from instruction.

People recognized that "equal opportunity" disappears if people have to pay individually for education. Opportunity is not equal if it sorts people into those who have money and those who don't. Thus charging tuition is a repudiation of democracy. Morrill's words "college training as a personal investment for profit" are meant to be a scathing criticism, something as bad as stealing. This perspective was sufficiently mainstream and dominant at that time to get written into law and implemented.

From "Education for Democracy" to training

Times have changed. Today, education for individual upward mobility is unquestioned. For-profit colleges, once restricted to a few trade schools, have branches in most US cities, are owned by large corporations and are traded on the stock market. Education "reform" movements push schools and colleges toward training for working class students and college and university educations for the lucky few. This narrow degree and credential training mission angers teachers and administrators who believe that their work in public education is fundamental to producing the educated citizenry who can participate in a democratic society.

The shift from education for democracy to education for profit happened bit by bit, over forty years, beginning in about 1974. That was the year when workers' wages and workers' productivity, which had been rising together since World War II, began to split apart. Productivity continued to climb upward, but wages sagged and then stalled and flattened. The result of this was loss of real wages, increased debt, more people working two jobs, more women and children in the workforce, and eventually, when people had maxed out their credit cards, loans on the equity in their houses. Tax rates also shifted, taking proportionally more from lower income brackets and less from the high end of the spectrum. Wealth was piling up for the 1%.

Then came the 2008 crash. People who had been laid off were going to have to be re-trained, but for what? In about 2010, the word "inequality" began to show up in the mainstream press. Increases in crime, mental illness, divorce, addiction and homelessness, which had been viewed as isolated social problems, were recognized as signs of rising inequality. The OCCUPY movement emerged in 2011. More and more people were asking, "What is education for?"

By then, it was not for an educated citizenry.

Now the people who defined what education was for were employers. Education is for job skills. Education can solve a skills shortage problem. The Workforce Investment Act of 1998 (WIA) was supposed to fund training for people being cut off public aid following welfare reform (the Personal Responsibility and Work Opportunity Reform Act of 1999).

WIA explicitly prioritized the needs of employers. Programs sprang up whenever there was a new or growing industry that needed trained workers: genetic coding, robotics, logistics, TV cable installation, new sub-fields in healthcare. Many of these jobs would only exist for a few years before they became obsolete. There was a boom in for-profit private schools that offered training in hot new fields.

Training does not solve the low-wage problem, however. It simply increases the number of people who will compete for low-wage jobs. Nor does it solve the unemployment problem, if people are graduating and there are no jobs.

It is easy to tell the difference between education and training. In training, students learn the curriculum. In education, students learn the curriculum and go on to critique and expand or change it. In training, students obey the instructor. In education, students are encouraged to overtake the teacher and go beyond what was expected in the class. In training, students are being prepared for a specific subordinate role in society, to work in someone else's business or institution. In education, the top is lifted off: they may look towards any role in society that they are capable of and choose their own horizon.

Representation in the education workplace

Schools and colleges are also workplaces. Teachers know what they need in order to do their jobs right. But good working conditions are rarely achieved without collective representation to carry what workers know about their work into the arenas where these conditions can be negotiated.

Teachers are, compared to other workforces, highly unionized. If you include the other public sector workers that are usually grouped with teachers (firefighters, police), they are over 40% unionized. Therefore they have the potential to build *communities of practice* and create *Work Process*

Knowledge. They have the potential for real democratic bottom-up problem solving. In the case of *public* education, however, the "bottom" includes more than just the teachers. The public has to be represented, too. This public is, like teachers themselves, predominantly working class.

Many big city schools no longer even have elected school boards: New York City, Cleveland, Baltimore, Boston, Philadelphia, Chicago and Detroit. These are all places where the tax base has plunged. The economic crisis leads to austerity budgets. Disasters create an opportunity to impose emergency management. Democracy goes out the window. Elected boards are fired and replaced with people appointed by mayors or governors. School systems get reorganized according to the ideals of people who are far from the classroom. Mega-foundations show up with plans that treat schools as businesses and measure "value" by test scores, graduation rates or even how much money their graduates earn.

Some reorganizations follow natural catastrophes, like the dismantling of the New Orleans Parish School Board following Hurricane Katrina in 2005, which left only four actual public schools and 70 state-run Recovery School District schools, all charter schools. In Chicago, elected boards of both schools and community colleges were eliminated by Mayor Daley under the guise of school reform.

The Chicago Teachers Strike, 2012

The city-wide strike of the Chicago Teachers Union in 2012 was a fight over whether *what* teachers know about their work should be considered in deciding *how* they do their work. The union and the school board had been negotiating for 9 months when the strike started.

According to an Illinois state law specifically written to affect Chicago, teachers in Chicago schools may not bargain over anything but wages and working conditions. Class size, resources for programs, the impact of testing, teacher evaluations, the availability of art and music, and school closures are all forbidden topics. For example, the teacher in Chapter 2 who taught biology out of the trunk of her car could not expect that the reasons why she needed a real biology lab would ever be discussed in negotiations. All the things that teachers know about their students, their community, their city and its history are off the table.

The strike exploded these limits because although the deadlock about wages was the legally-allowed occasion for the strike, the union made it clear that the real issues were not economic. This was well-understood by the public. Therefore the teachers had massive support, not only from teachers but also from parents, students and the city generally. Not one teacher crossed the picket lines at the nearly 700 schools. Parents and students marched with the teachers. The support made headlines. The result was a win. When the contract was signed, teachers got raises but they also kept teacher tenure and job security, established teacher control over lesson plans and won protections from bullying by principals plus the continuation of "Professional problems committee" which creates a way to negotiate with principals at the school level before filing a grievance. They won on issues they were supposedly forbidden to bargain over.

The public support of the union's issues were seen as a defeat for the now-national "reform" agenda (Sustar, 2013).

Looking back on the young people who wrote descriptions of their parents' involvement with their unions in Chapter 8, we can imagine what the dinner table conversations were like in Chicago in fall of 2012.

Laying the groundwork for this win, however, was a thirty-plus year job that involved many constituencies, not just the teachers. In preparing for the strike, teachers used what they know about how people learn: bottom-up and wide open, not secret, top-down or punitive. Most of that time, the center of the activist group was not in power in the union, the Chicago Teachers Union (CTU, IFT-AFT).

Back in 1989, the elected Chicago Public School Board was eliminated and replaced by appointees chosen by then Mayor Daley. The Board closed schools in Black and Latino neighborhoods and opened new magnet schools in white neighborhoods. They introduced a rigid standardized testing regime. The CTU leadership attempted to cooperate and agreed to concessions that over time sapped the strength of the union. For a decade, group of teachers led by George Schmidt had been putting out a newspaper called *Substance* that was critical of the Mayor but also relentlessly critical of the union leadership. Schmidt actually published some examples of the standardized tests in his newspaper, which got him fired.

In 2001, Latino parents started a hunger strike and an encampment in a poor neighborhood called Little Village demanding the construction of a high school. This strategy was dramatic, public and newsworthy. It got the attention of the new Superintendent, Arne Duncan, the same person who is now US Secretary of Education. Superintendent Duncan, who was on board for Daley's reform agenda, nevertheless released funds for the new high school.

By 2002 the critics of the union leadership managed to put forward a militant reform slate and won the union election. But the new president, Debbie Lynch, and the reformers were unable to build a sufficient base in the schools and among elected delegates. Lynch was defeated in the next election by an "old guard" candidate who was more willing to go along with the Mayor.

In 2004, Arne Duncan proposed a program called Renaissance 2010 which would have closed many Chicago schools and opened charter schools. In response, teachers started holding community meetings to discuss what this would mean. They were joined by the original *Substance* and the Debbie Lynch groups, others from a national network called Teachers for Social Justice and still more who had been involved in doing community education about the Renaissance 2010 program In 2008 this broad-based group formed a caucus called CORE, for Caucus of Rank and File Educators. They were not just teachers: they included other school employees like cafeteria workers, parents and community activists who had been campaigning against school closures.

They embarked on a long-term education, organizing and strategizing process. They held open forums, organized study groups and participated in book groups. The spirit of the Little Village hunger strike was still alive. Meetings were public, not limited to union members, and open in both their purpose and their membership. They also asked to have classes designed for them in the labor education program at the University of Illinois. These classes too were open to anyone. They did not keep people out or keep their purpose secret. They were building a *community of practice.*

From the beginning CORE talked about taking over the union and preparing for a big contract fight. As the next election approached, they looked for and found an articulate, energetic, outspoken teacher, Karen Lewis, who had been a high school chemistry teacher. They nominated her for union president at a large open convention.

CORE did not underestimate the challenge that lay ahead of them. Arne Duncan had moved on and was pushing the same agenda nationally that he had imposed in Chicago. The new Mayor, Rahm Emanuel, had just come from the Obama White House, where he had been Chief of Staff, famous for his dirty mouth and sudden rages. Where Mayor Daley had a certain rustic charm that he cultivated, Emanuel had none. He was known to be intolerant of dissent and easily angered and vindictive. Planning to strike the whole Chicago school system had to take into consideration facing Emanuel at his worst.

The outcome is history. In 2010 Karen Lewis was elected President of the CTU in a run-off. In a February 2014 Skype interview at a meeting held at City College of San Francisco, CTU Financial Secretary Kristine Mayle made it clear that the pressure to strike started in the schools, not among the leadership. The idea of wearing red on Fridays, as a sign of solidarity, spread among students and supporters including families. By now these were people who had been organized for years, through discussions, forums, study groups and rallies that focused on what education is for.

During the nine days of the strike the city belonged to the teachers and their supporters. Their red T-shirts created a theater of excitement on picket lines, in buses and on streets throughout the city.

As of this writing, Karen Lewis has survived one electoral challenge and CORE is still guiding the CTU. The union is still fighting school closings and charter schools but is now considering going directly into electoral politics by building a broad coalition around a program based on what the teachers know about their work, their communities and their city.

The Fight at City College of San Francisco (CCSF)

The final chapters of the fight at CCSF are yet to be written. But as of March 2014, the opinion of people watching the fight is that we are winning, with the caveat that we have not yet come to a full appreciation of the opposition. "I still can't really put a face on the enemy," says the young President of the faculty union, AFT Local 2121, Alisa Messer.

Both the Chicago and the San Francisco fights are stories of resistance to the education "reform" agenda. In Chicago, parents and teachers could see with their own eyes what happens when children spend too much time preparing for and taking standardized tests, when neighborhood schools get closed, when teachers lose their jobs, when charter schools get opened and teachers have no union representation. When the teachers fought to get back some control of their work, they did so at the bargaining table. The opposition sat across the table from them.

At San Francisco City College, the mechanisms of loss of student, teacher and community control are harder to see. However, the same foundations that try to remake our K-12 system are at work: The Walton Family Foundation, the Lumina Foundation, the Bill and Melinda Gates Foundations, the Joyce Foundation and others. They fund conferences, offer prizes, sponsor research, draft legislation, advise legislators at the state and federal level, write papers, provide consultants to advise institutions and give testimony at hearings. They provide trainings for college management. The resources they can muster exceed by many times the resources of the colleges they are trying to re-shape, to say nothing of the resources available to teachers. Although many of their materials say, "designed by teachers," they are not designed by the teachers of the classes where they will be used and do not respond to the actual conditions of their students. With multi-pronged campaigns, these organizations are steamrollers.

Except for the chosen few, by the time students are enrolled in post-secondary education, they are workers. Therefore top-down "reform" in higher education is all about teaching people to do what employers want them to do. According to the Clinton Global Initiative website, we must do something about "the mismatch between US business needs and America's access to the education and skills needed to secure a job." This means employer-defined learning outcomes and industry-recognized certificates, not degrees awarded on the basis of how many credits someone has taken in a given discipline.

As a result, "reform" is inevitably about loss of teacher control in the classroom. Learning outcomes must be predictable and testable. If there are five concurrent classes running where people learn, for example, psychology or biology, the learning outcomes have to be the same for all five no matter who the students are, what their backgrounds are, what their resources are or who the teacher is. These outcomes are called "SLO's," for "student learning outcomes". They are the higher education version of standardized tests. Teachers are evaluated on the basis of how well students do on tests based on these outcomes. The Educational Testing Service (ETS) already has a "suite" of tests for sale. What teachers know about students' learning is irrelevant.

"Reform" also means increasing the number of people who get degrees. Colleges will be judged successes or failures depending on how fast they move students to graduation. This is counter to the "lifelong learning" mission of community colleges. The Lumina Foundation's goal is to get 60% of Americans "high-quality" college degrees by 2025. The League for Innovation in the Community Colleges, a recipient of foundation funding, has a goal of getting twice as many students a degree at half the cost.

One way to do this is to put classes on line, use prepared learning outcome materials for class content, hire tutors or "coaches" rather than teachers to interact with students, and run huge classes. Although online classes can be good and even great learning experiences, it is a format that is easily degraded into a robotic tutorial-like experience.

To the general public, for whom the main issues are access and the price of tuition, "reform" can sound good and even exciting. There is a desperation market for classes, credentials and degrees, and as our economy shifts, as it will have to, the demand for these will only increase. Like health care, education is something people will pay for with their last dollar. There is therefore probably no limit to the profit that can be made out of this desperation market, and no limit to the damage.

The discourse of reform is full of phrases like "accountability," "do something different," "breakthrough learning mode," "student-centered learning," and "redesigning how students learn" that sound as if someone knows what they're doing. These phrases never go deeper than that. Nothing related to what we have been talking about in this book, about the kind of knowledge people need in order to be able to protect and improve their jobs and survive them, lessons about organizing for power in their workplaces, would make an appearance as a result of this line of reasoning. The most immediately apparent sign of this is that this learning is always seen as individual, not collective.

Instead, behind this appealing language is the value stashed away in public higher education that is ripe to be cashed in. For years K-12 schools have been shepherded into a market where testing companies, corporate charter schools and text book and software publishers can put a price on the value placed on education by families of children and teenagers. This is also happening in public higher education and adult education, which appear to be an undervalued commodity, ready for plucking. One symptom of this is the explosion of high-tuition for-profit colleges and universities. Looting the public sector is no longer considered a "betrayal of the American Dream," as it was in the 1960s.

City College: deep roots in the community

CCSF is the largest of the 112 California community colleges. It has deep roots in the community. It is over 75 years old and enrolls 100,000 students every semester. It has many programs that could easily be turned into profitable programs if they were closed at City College and opened at for-profit colleges. Its vocational programs in culinary arts, graphic design, construction, computer sciences and fashion marketing are intensive and well respected. It has a labor studies program, one of just a handful based in community colleges. Its vast adult education programs, which are tuition-free, serve tens of thousands in English as a Second Language (ESL), liberal arts, wellness, basic skills and cultural classes.

The community colleges in California are the living descendants of the 1960 California Master Plan for Higher Education. Despite pressures to increase tuition, California community colleges have remained low-cost and broadly accessible at $46 per credit. In 2013 a year's tuition, assuming 12 credits per semester, was about $1100. Although $46 per credit eliminates some students, it is not a ticket to crushing debt. However, many people remember when the first tuition fees were imposed in the 1980s. Even $6 per credit closed the doors for some students.

Nine neighborhood campuses are located throughout the city so that no one has to travel far to get to a class. Through the years of "do more with less" budgets, the college kept classes open by trimming from the top, protecting classes while cutting management. At least two thirds of the adult population of San Francisco has attended classes at CCSF. This was to be a critical factor in the fight.

Accreditation review comes to City College

The tool that was selected to do the work of the "reform agenda" for City College was the Accrediting Commission for Community and Junior Colleges, (ACCJC).

When the ACCJC began its review of CCSF in 2011, the faculty union, AFT2121, was wary but not ready for what was coming. The ACCJC had already lobbied for top-town "reforms" at the state level and built a track record of sanctions of other community colleges in its purview. These other colleges had, for the most part, responded by submitting to the Commission's demands. So the union did not expect the ACCJC to actually help, even though years of budget cuts had starved the college. Many institution-level needs at CCSF were openly acknowledged such as repair in infrastructure, maintenance, upgrading of computer systems, payroll and finances. The union did not expect ACCJC to recommend to the State Board of Governors that they release a new stream of funding to let the college get it back on its feet.

The union leadership was also concerned about the readiness of the union. At this point, it was an activist union, in the sense of having a progressive culture and supporting social justice generally. But it was not an internally well-organized union that was ready to fight.

AFT 2121 had been a strong union in the 1980s, when, because of the expanded hiring of adjuncts, it adopted the organizing culture necessary to bring the new hires into the union. During that decade the Union had had a series of important wins. An early example was a court case that established that adjuncts had the right to unemployment benefits between semesters and over the summer because they had no "reasonable assurance of employment." While preparing a court case is not necessarily a good internal organizing project, it served that purpose in this case because it required identifying and preparing a crowd of witnesses to cover every possible instance of the problem.

Following that win throughout the 1980's and 1990's, union elections brought increasingly strong leaders to the fore. Friends of the union were elected to the Board of Trustees. Union leaders became faculty senate leaders and sometimes administrators. Three union-friendly chancellors conducted bargaining using what is called "win-win," in which the union and the administration begin with the assumption that they have fundamentally shared concerns. AFT 2121 got the best contract in the country for adjunct community college faculty. Adjuncts not only had job security based on seniority, but also health benefits and 80% pro-rata pay. Unlike at other community colleges throughout the nation, even other colleges in California, a teacher at CCSF could actually live modestly on wages from adjunct teaching. In addition, CCSF had the highest percent of full-time faculty in the community college system. Because adjuncts had preference for hiring for those jobs, many of those people had been CCSF adjuncts. This meant that the level of tension between adjuncts and full-time faculty was relatively low. Former adjuncts were elected as union presidents.

Faculty took their good contract and their hard-won democratic governance institutions for granted. They did not understand them as fragile. The negative side effect of this was to demobilize the rank and file.

The ACCJC drops a bomb: "Show cause why CCSF should not be shut down."

After the year of review, on the Fourth of July weekend in 2012, the ACCJC announced that the college had one year to "show cause" why it should not be stripped of accreditation.

The impact of the announcement was like the impact of the "bomb" dropped by the Director of Heartland Health Services in Effingham, described in Chapter 7. For the workers at City College, responding to this bomb was going to be a first turn around *Kolb's Learning Cycle*.

People were shocked, confused and frightened. Wasn't this the very agency that was supposed to protect the quality of their work and their institution? Were they likely to lose their jobs after spending their entire professional lives here? Was this attack just the personal vendetta of the President of the ACCJC, Barbara Beno, who had had a mixed career in the community colleges?

Nothing in the ACCJC report criticized the quality of education provided by the college. The criticism was all about administrative structures (too much democratic shared governance) and finance (too many tenured faculty; too generous pay and benefits for adjuncts, not enough money in the reserves).

The recommendations of the ACCJC would make it easy to shrink the college and turn the vocational programs into employer-defined training programs. The academic programs would become gatekeeping transfer programs. The vast noncredit programs would disappear. This meant a complete change in the mission of the college and threatened the mission of the whole community college system.

A month after the "bomb," state-level union leader Marty Hittelman produced a research report, "ACCJC Gone Wild," in which he called ACCJC a "rogue" agency. Hittleman reported that under Beno's leadership, the ACCJC had issued 64% of all the 75 sanctions issued nationwide between June 2011 and June 2012. Later, another activist, Margaret Hanzimanolis, found out that when the ACCJC came to City College it had just received a three-year grant of $450,000 from the Lumina Foundation to explore a specific instrument for evaluating student learning outcomes called the DQP, or Degree Qualification Profile. Accrediting Commissions get their funding from dues from the various colleges that they review, plus some state funding. The Commission's umbrella organization, Western Association for Schools and Colleges (WASC), had similarly received a $1.5 million dollars grant for similar general "reform."

In this midst of the chaos, faculty set up working groups and joined teams to study the recommendations of the ACCJC, to decide what programs should be eliminated, what positions should be cut. They worked on SLO's. The attitude was basically, "Surely, these are reasonable people; maybe cooperating will turn out all right in the long run."

Meanwhile, students, community members and faculty formed a coalition called SaveOurCityCollege. They met, held demonstrations and marches, built a website, issued news bulletins, did sit-ins in the administration building, got arrested and made headlines.

In Fall 2012, the union, along with the elected Board of Trustees of the College, the Central Labor Council and other labor unions like SEIU, kicked off an initiative to go on the November 2012 ballot. The idea was that since so much of what could be criticized about the college was due to lack of money, raising money would fix those problems. Prop A, this initiative, called for a $79 per parcel tax on land in San Francisco. The explicit purpose of the money was "to keep classes open at City College." The effort to get this initiative onto the ballot engaged people from all different camps. To get signatures, people had to explain what had happened, what was true about the ACCJC report and what was wrong. Another proposition was also on the ballot, statewide Prop 30, which would raise money for public schools. Organizing for these initiatives and getting support for them after they were on the ballot made the whole city into a classroom in which a city-wide discussion was taking place.

Despite the national mood of "no new taxes," Prop A passed with the support of 73% of the voters. Prop 30 also passed. This stabilized the College's finances – theoretically. But soon after this, in January 2013, the administration cut faculty pay by 9%.

After the campaign to pass Prop A, the Union was in better shape. But it was far from being in shape to respond to the pay cut with a strike. The faculty union was not yet strong enough to do that.

The next learning experience was going to be a legal strategy. With the help of the state union, the California Federation of Teachers, AFT2121 filed an extensive complaint with the Department of Education alleging incompetence and conflicts of interest at the ACCJC. By now elected San Francisco City Supervisors were involved. When the ACCJC blocked faculty, media and the public from a public hearing, the fight began to get more support from the mainstream press.

Despite the year-long effort to cooperate with the ACCJC by participating in efforts to meet its demands, and despite the new money that was going to flow in from Prop A, the ACCJC dropped a new bomb in July 2013.

Bomb #2: Closing the College

In July 2013 the ACCJC announced that CCSF would lose its accreditation exactly one year later, in July 2014.

Up until now, it had been possible to say that perhaps there was some sense in the ACCJC's position and that cooperation might be rewarded. Now that possibility had been eliminated. "We have done what they wanted," was the feeling, "and it was all for nothing."

The "Special Trustee" who had been imposed on CCSF, Robert Agrella, was abruptly given total individual authority by the Board of Governors. He was empowered to make whatever changes he felt necessary. He fired the democratically elected Board of Trustees and replaced them with his "leadership team." Then he decided not to use the Prop A money to keep classes open, in spite of the promise that had been made to voters.

Looking at this moment through an *Activity theory* lens, you could say that people who had been in the middle, hoping to avoid the worst by cooperation, were now able to discern two activity systems in direct conflict. They saw that their cooperation had been fruitless. Now they had nothing to lose by joining fight back.

The union responded to the bomb with a massive campaign of phone calls and face to face meetings. The campaign had multiple purposes. One was to alert faculty to the likely loss of enrollment due to the threat to close the college. Loss of enrollment would mean a loss of state funding. Another was to generate turnout for a mass demonstration planned by the SaveCityCollege coalition. Another was to counter misinformation. A fourth was to help union members get to know each other and build the kind of commitment and reassurance that comes from being together with other people in a fight.

There were three main differences between the fight in Chicago and the fight in San Francisco. The first one was the timeline: decades in Chicago, a couple of years or less in San Francisco.

The second was the face of the opposition. The Chicago teachers went out on a contract strike over their control of their work. They knew who they were bargaining with. The City College faculty confronted a house of mirrors in which the enemy seemed to be an agenda. It was not a person on the other side of the table: it was an ideology.

After the July 2013 ACCJC shut-down announcement, the third difference between CCSF and the Chicago teachers became even more significant. CCSF had a great advantage over the Chicago teachers because unlike in Rahm Emanuel's Chicago, San Francisco's elected officials were, for the most part, natural CCSF advocates. Some had attended City College. The voter support for Prop A had sent a strong message. The Supervisors who represented districts with high proportions of recent immigrants knew how much their constituencies valued the adult education classes like ESL. When the Coalition and the Union were able to turn out thousands of people for a street demonstration, they noticed.

"Readiness" at the bargaining table

In August 2013, the tide seemed to start to turn. The mass

demonstration had filled the streets. The national AFT and state CFT sent staff support. A month after the ACCJC declared that the college would be shut down in July 2014, the U.S. Department of Education responded to the union complaint with a letter to the ACCJC saying it was out of compliance with its own standards.

With a sense that the mood of the City was behind them, and the perfidy of the Special Trustee and his appointees clearly visible, the Union leadership took steps to bring the fight home and focus on bargaining. Negotiations on the faculty contract had been stalled for months. It was time to adopt a stronger strategy. However, the union leadership knew that they did not have the kind of organizational strength required to pull off a successful strike. Therefore they had to choose a strategy that did not threaten a strike. The union made this decision in a large open meeting to which members who had participated in the fight up until now were invited.

They started by publicly dumping the win-win strategy as fruitless. In its place, they adopted a traditional adversarial bargaining stance. They told the administration that they would do "package" bargaining – that is, bargain over a whole proposed contract as a total package, not one item at a time. They argued that this would speed up bargaining. They also offered to do marathon bargaining, all day every day, in the hopes of getting the contract signed off before classes opened. They announced that future bargaining would take place in a "fishbowl," which means that all union members would be invited to sit in the room while negotiations were taking place. Members would not be allowed to talk, but their presence would validate and confirm that the union was doing its job of representation and negotiation.

This offer was both a show of resolve and readiness by the union, and a gesture of trust between the union and its membership. For people who had never seen bargaining before, it was an eye-opener.

The administration came to a few 12 and 16 hour bargaining sessions that were held as a "fishbowls." Then they walked out and declared impasse.

After mediation in September and October, the union and administration did sign a contract in November. This cleared the deck for the fight against the ACCJC.

Meanwhile, a cascade of official actions also took place, each on its own timeline. The legal strategy moved ahead. State Superintendent of Schools Tom Torlakson urged the ACCJC to rescind its decision. State senators called for an audit. The US Department of Education scheduled a December hearing in Washington, DC and the Union and SaveCCSF Coalition sent a delegation from CCSF to Washington, D.C. to give oral comments. At that meeting, the Department of Education put the ACCJC on notice to change its practices and to report back in a year. San Francisco City Attorney Dennis Herrera filed two legal actions against the ACCJC, one for unfair and illegal business practices and one against the State Chancellor's Office, charging them with delegating their responsibilities to an "unmonitored" entity. In December 2013, a hearing was held in San Francisco followed by an injunction granted in January 2014 to stop the ACCJC from carrying out its threat to shut down the college until the City Attorney's legal actions were concluded.

In other words, every official body, group or representative entity that could take a public position on defending City College did so (except the Mayor, Ed Lee, who unlike Rahm Emanuel stayed very quiet). Each in its own way, of course: the lawyers filed suits, the Union bargained, the Supervisors held hearings, the students demonstrated. There was a role for everyone and everyone joined in. These actions were publicized in all available media.

As of this writing, a bill has been submitted to the California State legislature that would clip the wings of the ACCJC and make it harder for foundations to use accreditation as their "reform" tool in the future. Some revelations about the fabulous salaries ($300,000 per year and more) of the Special Trustee and his appointees are making news. And the union is working to recover the College's democratically elected Board of Trustees.

In a fight like this, where does the learning take place?

The "bombs" put *Kolb's Learning Cycle* in motion. Organizing and high rates of participation revitalized the Union's *community of practice*. Debates and discussions on what Alisa Messer describes as problems on "three chessboards at once" produced decisions about what to do next, if not magic solutions. The reformers, although veiled by bureaucracies, revealed their agenda in a way that can be analyzed by *Activity Theory*. All of these theories of learning (with the exception of Kolb) assume that learning is social and collective.

Alisa Messer commented, "The hardest thing for the membership to learn is about how taking action together is important. Not just having an opinion, not just expressing that opinion well or even accurately, but taking action together."

She gave the following example. After the "fishbowl bargaining" sessions ended with the administration walking out, the Union decided to ask members to write letters to the Special Trustee to tell him why the administration should come back to the bargaining table and bargain in good faith. Getting faculty to write these letters was not easy. Many worried that their individual letters probably would have no impact. Others wanted to spend days refining the wording. It was hard to convince people that it wasn't any one individual letter that mattered, nor even what the letter said. As the letters started to come in, they were placed in a stack in a public place in the union office. The stack grew. People noticed. What convinced them was the stack. "It was the height of the stack of letters that communicated the message," said Messer. The stack of letters communicated power to the union members. They could picture how, when it was carried to the office of the Special Trustee, it would communicate power there, too.

Sometimes it is hard to explain how a tool "mediates" learning, as we say when we use Activity Theory. The height of the stack of letters makes a good example. The lesson of collective power could not come from reading or writing any one letter. No one said, "A big stack teaches me that my contribution to the collective fight is what matters." It came from the experience of contributing to the stack of letters and watching the stack grow higher.

Education for democracy?

If CCSF had been the kind of community college that the reformers envisioned, would it have been capable of this kind of fight back? A much smaller college devoted to preparing some students to transfer to the state universities and training others for employer-defined credentials? Obviously not. Years and years of keeping its doors open so that the majority of the people in the city passed through them made it possible, although not easy, for this fight back to happen.

But here is a question with a less obvious answer: In the case of San Francisco, many of the twists and turns of the story are about the crude mistakes made by the ACCJC or the Special Trustee, mistakes of hubris that could be avoided next time. If these mistakes are corrected for next time, will they be as easy to discern?

You can ask the same question about Chicago even more sharply. Just imagine a school system made of hundreds of isolated charter schools, comprising the whole spectrum of

231

inequality, with no teachers' union to represent a common ideal of how the work of teachers should be carried out. Could it mount any kind of fight back at all?

CHAPTER 14.:
"WHY DID I WRITE THIS BOOK?"

What did you learn in school today, dear little boy of
mine?
I learned our government must be strong
It's always right and never wrong...
— Tom Paxton

This is a book about labor education. Although some labor
education takes place in classes, most of it takes place on
the job, among people who have to learn on their own how
to push back against bad conditions at work. In this book,
I have taken four theories of learning and applied them to
work.

You might think that there would be many books about
this in the US. You might think that labor and education
would have a lot to say to each other. However, there is
virtually no discourse passing back and forth between labor
and education. This is in spite of the fact that most people go
to school and most people work.

When I say "education" I mean graduate schools of education, teacher training programs, policy institutes and the
major mainstream organizations that represent educators
and teachers. When I say "labor," I mean the mainstream labor organizations, progressive policy institutes, leaders and
staff. I do not mean labor educators.

Instead of a conversation, there is a wall between the world
of education and the world of labor. As someone who lives
and works in both worlds, I can describe this wall.

Education in the US does not think much about work or
the working class majority as workers. It does not want to
think about workers having to fight an employer. Labor
thinks very little about learning and even less about theory.

In fact, it avoids theory as much as possible.

The wall that keeps these two close cousins from talking to each other is historical. It is the result of two generations of effective popular campaigns against anything that seemed remotely Marxist. The fear of acknowledging class conflict makes education steer clear of ideas that take it as fundamental. The fear of being called "leftist" makes labor avoid anything that sounds like "theory." This explains why these theories, *Activity Theory* especially, are mainstream in other countries but not here. The forbidden lesson for us in the United States, in other words, is that there are theories that make sense of class conflict. They even make use of it.

Here are my suggestions for knocking a hole in this wall and getting some conversation going:

First: In order to understand how people learn at work, US educators should look at the specific social context where people are learning. This matters because the answer to the question, "Can they do that?" is specific to a particular country, state, sector, industry and even workplace. We need educators in the US who can write about learning at work in the US.

The leading practitioners and theorists who have published about adult learning and work are from outside the US. Few have approached adult learning with an understanding of the US workplace context.

Paulo Freire, the most famous and the foundational thinker of modern adult education, was from Brazil. Michael Newman is from Britain and Australia. Roger Simon, Don Dippo and Arlene Schenke are Canadian, as are Peter Sawchuk, Sue Carter and D'Arcy Martin. Yrjo Engeström is Finnish. Knud Illeris is Danish. Stephen Billet is Australian. Jean Lave, whose influential work is on communities of practice, talks about work in the US and is from the US, but her most significant examples are from overseas.

Of all adult education practitioners in the US who write

about learning and work, Myles Horton stands out, and this is probably because he personally worked on both sides of the wall in his own lifetime. He was an educator for the Congress of Industrial Organizations (CIO) and an organizer among textile workers in North and South Carolina in the 1930s. He also started the Highlander Center, which played an important education role in the Civil Rights movement. Sylvia Scribner is another exception who worked on both sides of the wall: she was not only an education academic, but also a union staff person and educator. But their work was done many decades ago.

Social relationships in different places and at different times are different because their norms, rules, laws and histories (see *Activity Theory*) are different. Labor and employment laws in the US are different from those in Brazil, Britain, Canada, Finland, and other countries. Not only that, every state in the US has different labor laws for the public sector, and some have none at all. Unionized workplaces are governed by contracts as well as labor law. This means that the social relationships in all these places are different.

Since "social relationships" include who can do what to whom in the starkest sense, theorizing learning about work without an appreciation of the concrete social relations of work fails to account for the essence of learning in context. Think about how different the social relationships of Heartland Health Services in Effingham were after the contract.

Second: Labor education should be a required part of job training. When labor looks at education, we see that the study of learning at work is overwhelmed by the job training agenda. The purpose of the job training agenda is to make people employable and productive, which is not the same as raising their labor standards and enabling them to control their work lives. This agenda includes adult literacy, numeracy, the whole range of "skills" from hard to soft, self-presentation, how to dress and speak, attitude and of course, assessment and testing. It includes the recently multiplying "professional" graduate schools. Adult education also has a tradition of general education and liberal arts, but they are not about work. Poems and stories, even if they are working-class poems and stories, are not directly about the social relations of work.

Third, do not confuse workplace justice with broad social justice. The most profound thinkers about adult education in the US, people like Willie Baptist, Ira Shor, Mike Rose, Henry Giroux and Smokey Wilson, are focused on society in general and the lives and life chances of the poor. A general term for their perspective is "critical pedagogy." They are in step with the great liberation educators of Central and Latin America. However, they don't talk about the specific conditions of work in this country. It is one thing to be critical of neoliberalism or free-market capitalism. It is another to get down to the specifics of how people get together, think about problems, communicate their ideas to others, and then act collectively in the face of threats to their ability to earn a living.

Even the most progressive movement-based social justice adult education practice fails by not dealing with the arrangements that bring workers and employers face-to-face to negotiate how hard people have to work and what they will get paid for it.

Fourth, the social sciences are not the only disciplines that are important for workers who are trying to organize. The social sciences – history, sociology, political science, for example – are not applied. You learn about things, you don't practice doing things. The final exam in a history class rarely includes changing the laws that govern your own people, thereby changing the course of their history. Education, although it is partly philosophy, is an applied field. You take a theory into a situation and you try it and if it doesn't work, you try another one.

Mainstream labor history avoids being applied when it is just a stream of narratives: A great leader *organized* people, unions *recruited* members, workers *went on strike*, they *fought* the police or the Guard, they *went to jail*, they *negotiated* a contract, they *elected* a new board. The story is told with action verbs and direct objects. How a workforce *learned* to organize itself, or the lessons they learned while doing it, is rarely examined. The learning is skipped as the story moves along.

An exception to the claim that labor history does not concern itself with how people learn is Frank Bardacke's book *Trampling Out the Vintage: Cesar Chavez and the Two Souls of the United Farm Workers* (Verso 2012). He explicitly addresses how a workforce learned how to achieve control of its own work. But Bardacke himself is an adult educator and spent many years teaching adult school in Watsonville, California; he is unusually conscious of how adults learn.

Fifth and last: Class conflict is fundamental to the experience of work under capitalism. Labor acknowledges this. Labor educators teach about how to participate in a fight. The foundations named in Chapter 13 do not. The world of school learning does not. Adult education, as a field, tries to avoid thinking about it (individual adult educators can't avoid it).

The wall between education and labor cuts the primary experience of adult life, work, in two. It disrespects the actual experience of ordinary people. In fact, it literally silences them by cutting them in half. It freezes discussion and guarantees the failure of fights to reduce inequality. All that "making a living" means, and how to achieve it in terms of wages, working conditions, safety, security, dignity and surviving the job, and the likely need to fight to make this happen, is blanked out. Yet the same people who come to schools looking for adult education are likely to be the best equipped, morally and mentally, for joining the fight. On the flip side, the same people who come to work looking for a way to make a decent living should be the best equipped with the knowledge of how to do it.

Forbidden lessons

I wish there was a simple name to the kind of learning that I have talked about in this book. I can't do better than the name in the title of the book: Forbidden lessons.

The word "lessons" – instead of knowledge or learning –reminds us that we are talking about something that has to be learned in practice, over and over again. It is always new in each new situation. This is because the fundamental conflict between the interests of employers and workers is never resolved.

The word "forbidden" reminds us that we are talking about a specific social context, the social relations of work in our liberal democracy at this moment in capitalism. We are talking about a conversation that has to take place through a wall. Our context requires that these lessons be suppressed, distorted, or forbidden as much as possible.

Theory itself is a tool that can bring these lessons out into the light of day.

Kolb's Learning Cycle will help us be patient while people absorb an experience and figure out how to respond. The cycle may be a matter of minutes or months. Lave's *Communities of Practice* will help us think about how people are introduced to a struggle or an existing organization, whether it is a union or something else. It will help us identify actions that exclude or delegitimize newcomers, putting the long-term survival of the community at risk. It will help us identify good ways to bring people into a struggle. It will give us tests we can use to evaluate the longevity of a collective. *Work Process Knowledge* theory makes us look at problems as opportunities, and guides us to pull people together to solve them and communicate with they learn to others. It encourages horizontal communication rather than hierarchical communication and tolerates wild ideas. *Activity Theory* forces us to focus on purpose. It helps us identify who is on our side and who has a significantly different purpose. It can serve as a kind of checklist to evaluate where conflicts or shifts are likely to take place. It helps us figure out what tools we need to acquire or create and what laws, customs or standards we are operating under. It requires us to look ahead to prepare for what may happen if we succeed or fail.

What these theories have in common (even *Kolb's Learning Cycle*, the way I am using it) is that they explain how people learn collectively. They are about people getting together under difficult conditions and figuring out how to fight back in a way that will benefit them all. They are not about individual upward mobility or individual achievement. They are about reducing, not increasing, inequality.

In Chapter 5 I noted that the two great thinkers who developed the ideas that lie at the roots of these theories, Vygotsky and Freire, did so in the context of societies that were undergoing profound change. Today, we live in a global society that is undergoing profound change. As of right now, we – that is, workers - do not have a theoretical tool, much less a political strategy, with which to harness and control that change. In the meantime, the direction of change is towards increasing inequality, harsher differences, tougher fights.

And as of now, these lessons are still forbidden.

ACKNOWLEDGEMENTS

Many organizations and individuals contributed to my thinking through of the ideas in this book. Hopefully, this process will continue. I appreciate all kinds of communications about how other people understand learning at work. I can be reached at hworthen@illinois.edu.

Thanks to my students at the National Labor College, especially those with whom I worked on their Prior Learning Assessment portfolios. Writing an "education resume" forces a person to review one's entire work history and identify what was learned, good or bad, at each job.

Thanks to the Education Department at the American Federation of State, County and Municipal Workers (AFSCME) for giving me access to the essays of high school seniors applying for the AFSCME Family Scholarship.

Thanks to the Center for Democracy in a Multi-Racial Society at the University of Illinois, which funded the interviews of job-seekers in Chapter 9. Some of this material was first published in Worthen, H. and Haynes, Rev. A. (2003). "Getting In: The Experience of Minority Graduates of the Building Bridges Project Pre-Apprenticeship Class." *Labor Studies Journal.* Vol. 28, 1. pp. 31-52 and Worthen, H. and Haynes, A. (2009). A Comparison of the Outcomes of Two Pre-Apprenticeship Programs. *Journal of Community Practice,* 17, 1-2, pages 207-222.

Thanks to the International Brotherhood of Electrical Workers, IBEW Local 134 for making it possible to interview third-year apprentices about their on-the-job field experience. Material in that was excerpted from these interviews and appears in Chapter 9 was previously published in Worthen, H. and Berchman, M. (2010). Apprenticeships: What goes on in On-The-Job Training (OJT)? Chapter 12, pp 222-239 in Billett, ed. *Learning through practice: Models, traditions, orientations and approaches.* Dordrecht, DE: Springer

Thanks to the Trustees of the Regina Polk Fund for Women's Labor Leadership, who funded annual multi-day women's conferences and enabled me to develop curriculum in ways not easily done under ordinary conditions;

Thanks to my colleagues at the United Association for Labor Education (UALE), which holds annual conferences where I have been able to present some of these ideas, including material in Chapter 5 which was first published as Worthen, H. (2011). CHAT Learning Theory for Labor Educators: Work Process Knowledge, Activity Theory, and Communities of Practice in *Labor Studies Journal*, 36:4, p. 538-544 and Worthen, H. (2008), Using Activity Theory to Understand How People Negotiate the Conditions of Work, in *Mind, Culture and Activity*, 15: 4.

Thanks to the Grievance Division of the National Writers Union, for being a real community of practice. Working with the GD put me in a position to witness how twenty years of changes in technology have transformed the economic relationship between writers and readers;

In addition, I would like to thank the following people as individuals:

Nancy Augustine, shop chair at Osan's in Boyertown, Pennsylvania;

Betty Barrett , project director for the power plant study;

Mark Berchman, the IBEW journeyman and apprenticeship instructor who did many of the interviews with apprentices for that chapter;

Joe Berry, without whom this book (and a lot of other things) would have never been written;

Emanuel Blackwell, who did many of the interviews for Chapter 9 on apprenticeships and who was the math teacher who made it possible for all our Building Bridges graduates to pass the Carpenter's entrance test;

Andy Blunden, at Marxists.org and editor, organizer and author;

Jerome Bruner, who assigned Vygotsky's *Thought and Language* to his students at Harvard in 1961;

Mike Cole at UC San Diego, moderator of the XMCA Mind, Culture and Activity list serve and tireless supporter of people with questions and ideas;

Karen Ford, journalist and National Writers Union organizer, who tracked down the Building Bridges graduates, persuaded them to let her interview them, and wrote up the interviews;

Jocelyn Graf, research assistant, editor and friend;

Norton Grubb, for his support while I was working on my dissertation at U. C. Berkeley School of Education;

Margaret Hanzimanolis, for her research into the foundation funding behind the post-secondary "reform" agenda;

Rev. Anthony Haynes, Director of the Building Bridges Project, from whom I learned the most while we were in Chicago;

Ed Hertenstein, colleague at the University of Illinois Labor

Education Program, who worked on the Effingham study;

Glynda Hull, who introduced me to Engeström, Activity Theory and CHAT while I was taking her classes at U. C. Berkeley;

Elissa McBride, Education Director for AFSCME, who oversaw the Family Scholarship program;

Susan Schacher, grassroots activist and adult basic education teacher in Oakland, California;

Tim Sheard, friend, fellow NWU member, and owner of Hard Ball press;

Irv Rosenstein, mentor at UNITE in Philadelphia;

Gail Warner, Azure Newman, Lucille Musser, and Anna Beck, leaders in the Effingham struggle;

And Hilary Worthen, my brother, who said, upon reading an early draft, "From a management perspective, this is a disaster."

READINGS AND REFERENCES

This list includes both my sources for the ideas in this book and additional readings for people who want to find out what lies behind those ideas. Some of these are written for use in labor education classes or social movement workshops. Others are written for an audience of academics. It is in keeping with my goals for this book that writing for both audiences be combined into one list.

Arnold, R., Burke, B. James, C. Martin, D. & Thomas, B. (1991) *Education for a Change*. Toronto, Ontario: Between the Lines and The Doris Marshall Institute for Education and Action.

Aronowitz, S. (1973) Lordstown: Disruption on the Assembly Line, Chapter 1 (p. 21-50) in *False Promises: The Shaping of American Working Class Consciousness*. New York, NY: McGraw-Hill

Bardacke. F.(2012) *Trampling Out the Vintage: Cesar Chavez and the Two Souls of the United Farmworkers*. New York, NY: Verso

Barkan, J. (2014) "How Mega-Foundations Threaten Public Education," p. 73-88 in *Class Action: An Activist Teacher's Handbook*. Jacobin Magazine, www.jacobinmag.org. NY: Jacobin Foundation

Billet, S. (Ed.). (2010) *Learning Through Practice: Models, traditions, orientations and approaches*. New York, NY: Springer Science+Business Media

Blunden, A. (2014) *Collaborative Projects: An Interdisciplinary Study*. Leiden: Brill

Boreham, N.; Fischer, M.; & Samurçay, R. (2002). *Work Process Knowledge.* New York, NY: Routledge

Bransford, J.D.; Brown, A.L.; Cocking, R.R. (Eds). (2000) *How People Learn: Brain, Mind, Experience, and School.* Committee on Learning Research and Educational Practice, National Research Council

Bruner, J. (1986) *Actual Minds, Possible Worlds.* Cambridge, MA: Harvard University Press

Burroughs, E.R. (1963) [1912] *Tarzan of the Apes.* New York, NY: Ballentine Books

California State Department of Education. (1960) *A Master Plan for Higher Education in California, 1960-1975* http://www.ucop.edu/acadinit/mastplan/MasterPlan1960.pdf

Cole, M. (1996) *Cultural Psychology: A once and future discipline.* Cambridge, MA: Harvard University Press

Dannin, Ellen. April 23, 2012. Permission to use text of *Petition on Behalf of Kate Bronfenbrenner*

Diaz-Cabrera, D., Hernandez-Fernaud, E. & Isla-Diaz, R. An evaluation of a new instrument to measure organizational safety culture values and practices. *Accident analysis and prevention* 39 (2007) 1202-1211

Engestrom, Y. (1987) *Learning by Expanding: an activity-theoretical approach to developmental research.* Helsinki: Orienta-Honsultit

Engestrom, Y. (2001) Expansive Learning at Work: toward an

activity theoretical reconceptualization. *Journal of Education and Work*, Vol 14. 2001. p 133-156

Freire, P. (1992) [1992] *Pedagogy of the Oppressed*. New York, NY: Continuum

Freire, P. (1985) *The Politics of Education: Culture, Power and Liberation.* South Hadley, MA: Bergin and Garvey

Gardner, H. (1987) *The Mind's New Science: A History of the Cognitive Revolution.* New York, NY: Basic Books

Giroux, H. (2013) America's Education Deficit and the War on Youth. New York, NY: Monthly Review Press

Greenhouse, S. (4.14.2012) Employers Don't Have to Post Union Notices, Judge Rules. *New York Times.* B7

Greenhouse, S. (12.11.2013). Study Finds Federal Contracts Given to Flagrant Violators of Labor Laws *New York Times*, p B1,B2,

Grote, G. & Kunzler, C. (2000) Diagnosis of safety culture in safety management audits. *Safety Science 34* (2000) 131-150

Grubb, W.N. (1996) *Learning to Work: The case for reintegrating job training and education.* New York, NY: Russell Sage

Hittleman, M. (2013). *ACCJC Gone Wild.* http://www.saveccsf.org/wp-content/uploads/2013/05/ACCJC-GoneWild-v13.pdf

Horton, M. (1990) *The Long Haul: An Autobiography.* With Judith Kohl and Herbert Kohl. New York, NY: Doubleday

Human Engineering. (2005) *A review of safety culture and*

safety climate literature for the development of the safety culture inspection toolkit. Research Report 367. Health & Safety Executive, Shore House, 68 Westbury-on-Trym, Bristol, BS93AA

Hutchins, E. (1995) *Cognition in the Wild*. Cambridge, MA: MIT University Press

Illeris, K. (2002) *The Three Dimensions of Learning: Contemporary leaning theory in the tension filled between the cognitive, the emotional and the social*. DK: Roskilde University Press

Illeris, K. (Ed.). (2009). *Contemporary Theories of Learning: Learning theorists...in their own words*. New York, NY: Routledge

Illeris, K. (2004). *Adult Education and Adult Learning*. Malabar, Florida: Krieger Publishing Company. Originally published 2003 in Denmark by Roskilde University Press

Kardas, P.A. (2009) *Cutting the Heart out of the Labor Center: A Response to an audit by Maryam Jacobs, TESC Internal Auditor* by Peter A. Kardas, Director TESC Labor Education and Research Center. Available from Sarah Laslett, Director, Washington State Labor Education and Research Center at South Seattle Community College

Kolb, D. A. (1984) *Experiential Learning: Experience as the source of learning and development*. Englewood Cliffs, NJ: Prentice Hall.
URL: http://www.learningfromexperience.com/images/uploads/process-of-experiential-learning.pdf! (31.05.2006)

Kolbert, E. (2013) *The Sixth Extinction: An Unnatural History*. New York, NY: Henry Holt and Co.

Lafer. G. (2002) *The Job Training Charade*. Ithaca, NY: Cornell University Press

Larson, S. & Nissen, B. Eds. (1987) *Theories of the Labor Movement*. Detroit; MI: Wayne State University Press

Laslett, S. (April 23, 2012) *Landmark's Requests and Labor Center Responses. Table with eleven entries*. Provided by Sarah Laslett, Director Washington State Labor Education and Research Center at South Seattle Community College.

Lave, J. (1988) *Cognition in Practice: Mind, Mathematics and Culture in Everyday Life*. New York, NY: Cambridge University Press

Lave, J. (1996) Teaching, as Learning, in Practice. *Mind, Culture and Activity*. Vol. 3, No. 3. p. 149-164

Lave, J. (1991) *Situating Learning in Communities of Practice*. Chapter 4 p. 63-82 in Resnick, L.B.; Levine, J.M.; & Teasley, S.D. (Eds.) Perspectives on Socially Shared Cognition. Washington, DC: American Psychological Association

Lave, J. & Wenger, E. (1991) *Situated Learning: Legitimate Peripheral Participation*. New York, NY: Cambridge University Press

Leont'ev, A.N. (1978) *Activity, Consciousness and Personality*. Englewood Cliffs, NJ: Prentice-Hall

Livingstone, D. W. (2004) [1999] *The Education-Jobs Gap: Underemployment or Economic Democracy*. Aurora, Ontario: Garamond Press

Livingstone, D.W. & Sawchuk, P. H. (2003) *Hidden Knowledge: Organized Labor in the Information Age.* Lanham, MD: Rowan and Littlefield

Loewen, J. (1995) Lies my Teacher Told Me: Everything your American History Textbook Got Wrong. New York, NY: The New Press

Loewen, J. (1999) *Lies Across America: What Our Historic Markers and Monuments Get Wrong.* New York, NY: The New Press

Lopes, T, & Thomas, B. (2006) *Dancing on Live Embers: Challenging Racism in Organizations.* Toronto, ON: Between the Lines

Malanga, S.. August 13, 2003. *Picketing 101.*Wall Street Journal
http://online.wsj.com/article/0,,SB106073910489790800,00.html

Martin, D. (1995) *Thinking Union: Activism and Education in Canada's Labour Movement.* Toronto, Ontario: Between the Lines

Newman, M. (1994) *Defining the Enemy: Adult Education in Social Action.* Paddington, NSW: Stewart Victor Publishing

Newman, M. (1993) *The Third Contract: Theory and Practice in Trade Union Training.* Paddington, NSW: Stewart Victor Publishing

Newman, M. (1999) *Maeler's Regard: Images of Adult Learning.* Paddington, NSW: Stewart Victor Publishing

Parker, D., Lawrie, M., Hudson, P. A framework for understanding the development of organizational safety culture. *Safety Science* 44 (2006) 551-565

Perrow, C. (2007) *The Next Catastrophe: Reducing our Vulnerabilities to Natural, Industrial and Terrorist Disasters.* Princeton, NJ: Princeton University Press

Piercy, M. (1980) *The Low Road*, from "The Moon is Always Female." New York, NY: Knopf

Pihlaja, J. (2005) *Learning in and for Production: An activity-theoretical study of the historical development of distributed systems of generalizing.* Doctoral dissertation, University of Helsinki, Faculty of Behavioral Sciences, Department of Education https://oa.doria.fi/handle/10024/3665

Reason, J. 1997. *Managing the Risks of Organizational Accidents.* Ashgate, Aldershot

Reich, R. (1992) *The Work of Nations: Preparing ourselves for 21st Century Capitalism.* New York, NY: Knopf

Reiman, T., Oedewald, P.; & Rollenhagen, P. September 2005. *Reliability Engineering & System Safety.* Vol 89. p 331-345

Richardson, C. (2007) Work Restructuring and Employee involvement: Watching Out for the Tricks and traps. http://charleyrichardson.org/ and on the University of Massachusetts Lowell Labor Extension's website at http://www.uml.edu/LaborEducation/Publications/Fact-Sheets.aspx or http://charleyrichardson.org/labor/wp-content/uploads/2011/10/TRICKS-3-07.pdf

Rogalski, J.; Plat, M.; & Antolin-Glenn, P. 2002. Training for collective competence in rare and unpredictable situations. P. 134-147, Chapter 10 in *Work Process Knowledge,* Boreham, N.; Fischer, M.; & Samurcay, R., editors. NY: Routledge

Rose, M. (1989) *Lives on the Boundary: A Moving Account of the Struggles and Achievements of America's Educational Underclass.* New York, NY: Penguin

Rose, M. (2004) *The Mind at Work: Valuing the Intelligence of the American Worker.* New York, NY: Viking

Sawchuk. P. (2003) *Adult Learning and Technology in Working-Class Life.* Cambridge, UK: Cambridge University Press

Scribner, S. 1997. *Part V, Thinking at Work, in Mind and Social Practice: Selected Writings of Sylvia Scribner.* Ethel Tobach, Rachel Joffe Falmagne, Mary B. Parlee, Laura M. W. Marting, Aggie Scribner Kapelman, Editors. Cambridge University Press: NY, NY

Shor, I. (1980) Critical Teaching and Everyday Life. Boston: South End Press

Simon, R.I.; Dippo, D.; & Schenke, A. (1991) *Learning Work: A Critical Pedagogy of Work Education.* Toronto, ON: OISE Press

Smith, A. 1993 [1776]. *The Wealth of Nations.* Sutherland, K (Ed) Reading, Berkshire: Oxford University Press

Sustar, L. "Will teachers keep moving forward?" http://www.substancenews.net/articles.php?page=4240&section=Article

US Chemical Safety and Hazard Investigation Board. March 2007. *Investigation Report Vinyl Chloride Monomer Explosion (5 dead, 3 injured, and community evacuated) Formosa Plastics Corp,*

Illiopolis, Illinois April 23, 2004. Report No. 2004-10-I-IL

US Court of Appeals, Fourth District. Chamber of Commerce vs National Labor Relations Board http://www.ca4.uscourts.gov/opinions/Published/121757.p.pdf

US Department of Labor   (1999) *Report on the American Workforce*

Virkkunen, J. (2007) Collaborative development of a new concept for an activity. @ctivites, 4 (2), pp 158-164

Vygotsky, L. S., (1934/1987) 'Thinking and Speech', *Collected Works*, Volume 1, p. 39–285, New York: Plenum Press

Vygotsky, L.S. (1962) *Thought and Language.* Translated by Eugenia Hanfmann and Gertrude Vakar. Cambridge, MA: MIT Press

Vygotsky, L. S. (1978) *Mind in Society: The Development of Higher Psychological Processes.* Edited by M. Cole, V. John-Steiner, S. Scribner and Ellen Souberman. Cambridge, MA: Harvard University Press

Ward, C.O. (1888, 1900) *The Ancient Lowly: A history of the ancient working people from the earliest known period to the adoption of Christianity by Constantine.* Chicago: Kerr. Available on line.

Westrum, R. 1996. Human factors experts beginning to focus on organizational factors in safety. *ICAO Journal* (October)

Westrum, R. (2004) A typology of organisational cultures. *Qual Saf Health Care* 2004;13 (Suppl II):ii22–ii27. doi:10.1136/qshc.2003.009522

Wilson, S. (2007) "What about Rose?" Using Teacher Research to Reverse School Failure. New York, NY: Teachers College Press

Yancey, T. (2013) ACCJC Facts and Analysis. Backgrounder from Save CCSF/Fight Back. kolsyk@gmail.com.

Zohar, D. 1980. Safety climate in industrial organizations: theoretical and applied implications. *Journal of Applied Psychology* 65 (1), 96-102

Zook, G. and American Council on Education. (1947) *Higher Education for Democracy: A Report of the President's Commission on Higher Education.* New York: Harper Bros. http://courses.education.illinois.edu/eol474/sp98/truman.html

INDEX

ABOUT THE AUTHOR

Helena Worthen taught writing at the college level until she realized that what her students needed most was decent jobs. After completing her PhD at the University of California Graduate School of Education she drew on her experience with the California Federation of Teachers (AFT/AFL-CIO) and became a labor educator. She worked for UNITE, the National Labor College, and the University of Illinois School of Labor and Employment Relations, from which she retired in 2010. She lives in Berkeley, California with her husband, Joe Berry. She can be reached at hworthen@illinois.edu.

TITLES FROM HARD BALL PRESS

NEW YORK HUSTLE - Pool Rooms, School Rooms & Street Corners, by Stan Maron

MANNY AND THE MANGO TREE, a children's story by Ali & Valerie Bustamante, Illustrated by Monica Lunot-Kuker

LOVE DIES, A Thriller, by Timothy Sheard

MURDER OF A POST OFFICE MANAGER,
A Legal Thriller, by Paul Felton

SIXTEEN TONS,
An Historical Novel, by Kevin Corley

WHAT DID YOU LEARN AT WORK TODAY? THE FORBIDDEN LESSONS OF LABOR EDUCATION, nonfiction, by Helena Worthen

WITH OUR LOVING HANDS Nursing Home Workers Tell Their Story

The Lenny Moss Mysteries, by Timothy Sheard

THIS WON'T HURT A BIT

SOME CUTS NEVER HEAL

A RACE AGAINST DEATH

SLIM TO NONE

NO PLACE TO BE SICK

A BITTER PILL

SOMEONE HAS TO DIE (coming in 2015)

Made in the USA
Middletown, DE
10 May 2022